Big Trouble Coming

DASHA ROSS

BIG TROUBLE COMING

Big Trouble Coming

An accidental adventure of love and mayhem in Sri Lanka

DASHA ROSS

Valentine Press

Published in 2024 by Valentine Press

Copyright © 2024 by Dasha Ross

All rights reserved. No part of this book may be reproduced or transmitted in any form or by any means, electronic or mechanical, including photocopying, recording or by any information storage and retrieval system, without prior permission in writing from the publisher. The Australian Copyright Act 1968 allows a maximum of one chapter or 10 percent of this book, whichever is the greater, to be photocopied by any educational institution for its educational purposes.

Valentine Press
20 Fotheringham Street
Enmore 2042
www.valentinepress.com.au

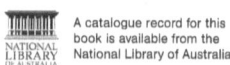

A catalogue record for this book is available from the National Library of Australia

ISBN: 9780987506351
Cover design: Design by Committee
Author photograph: Tim Bauer

Printed and bound by Ingram Spark

First published, 2024

Foreword

This is a 'true' story based on actual incidents and real people my husband, John Pinder, and I met when we worked together to refurbish and relaunch a hotel on a surf beach in south west Sri Lanka.

We lived it. We loved it. We might have died, but we didn't. It all happened, but the telling of this story is my interpretation of the events.

I've changed some people's names to protect their privacy. But not all. Some characters are composites for the sake of storytelling.

The sources I've relied on are primarily my notes, my interviews with people who were present at the time, and the numerous books mentioned in the acknowledgements. But the richest vein of gold was Google Mail, which stored all the emails we sent at the time. This digital diary provided much detail, including what was said at the time and what we did when.

For my ringmaster

Contents

Foreword vii
Dedication viii

1	UP IN SMOKE	1
2	SERENDIPITY	4
3	WALL OF DEATH	11
4	COME ON OVER	18
5	ARRIVAL	25
6	NALINDA	34
7	THE COUNTDOWN BEGINS	40
8	FIVE WEEKS TILL SHOWTIME	44
9	TICK TOCK ON THE CLOCK	52
10	THREE WEEKS TO GO	61
11	BLOW THE HOUSE DOWN	72
12	TOO MANY COOKS	75
13	THE TEMPERATURE'S RISING	88
14	AT LAST	92
15	FAULTY PALMS	97

16	NO. 3 HOTEL	110
17	THE BARMY ARMY	122
18	HAPPY NEW YEAR	130
19	GLOVES OFF	134
20	SUNSET SHOWDOWN	142
21	EXIT STAGE LEFT	153
22	I'VE DONE IT ALL	160
23	HIS SPIRIT LIVES ON	169
24	ACKNOWLEDGEMENTS	176

ABOUT THE AUTHOR   179

Chapter 1

UP IN SMOKE

Perfection. Or so it seemed.

The setting, the negroni cocktails reflecting the colours of the sunset, and our rekindled love for each other after 25 years of marriage.

Cue Lou Reed, 'Oh, such a perfect day'.

'Looks like we've pulled it off,' toasted my husband, lifting his glass.

We clinked glasses, soaking up the pleasure of Colombo's Galle Face Hotel. An iconic location that oozed history, from the genteel colonial formality of the 1800s to wild 21st century gun fights involving the offspring of Sri Lanka's modern power elite.

I couldn't imagine a better place to celebrate our quixotic Sri Lankan adventure. From our hotel room's balcony, we watched the sky spin from day to night as the sun dropped behind the horizon, a giant vermillion ball melting into the Indian Ocean. In front of us, the sunset colours changed, intensified and deepened again. As the sky morphed into darkness, I felt a nameless unease prickle under my skin. The sunset's evanescence reminded me how fleeting perfection can be.

My phone perforated our reverie.

'Dasha, where are you?'

'In Colombo. Where I said we'd be.'

'Stay there. Nalinda says he wants to kill John! You've got to stay where you are. You can't go back there,' Nick barked from half a world away.

Frozen, I passed the phone to John.

'But Nick, all our stuff's there. Passports, money. And our friends are coming from Australia tomorrow, so we have to go back.'

'You can't. Not till things calm down.'

Beads of sweat illuminated the top of John's head. Our eyes locked silently; the first time I'd ever seen him lost for words in our marriage.

I collapsed in the nearest chair, 'Now what?'

John gazed into the distance, his best poker face framed by his oversized signature yellow glasses.

Hardly a fitting finale to our eight months as boutique hotel managers. Not the one we anticipated. But in the light of recent events, neither could I say entirely unexpected.

'Do you reckon Nalinda's for real?" I ask.

'Who knows,' shrugged John, 'it's impossible to know what he's thinking. But one thing we do know is that anything's possible here.'

Later we stood distracted and shaken on a downtown Colombo street, joining the throngs of people watching the glorious Buddhist Perahera Parade. This event brought us to Colombo and we were determined not to miss it.

A hundred elephants cloaked in a rainbow of sequined burqas ambled through the sticky night air, hobbled by ankle chains. They passed by, accompanied by the rhythmic beating of hundreds of drums, packs of dancers stomping their feet, stilt walkers towering over the crowd, and posses of fire twirlers spinning their flaming sticks – a dazzling eruption of colour and sound. As the decibels rose and the dancers twirled faster, the phone call kept whirring and looping like windmills in my mind.

How could our dream of paradise turn so bad so quickly?

Chapter 2

SERENDIPITY

Serendib is the ancient trading name for Sri Lanka, and it truly was serendipity that brought us to live on this beguiling island.

We didn't plan on going there; we didn't plan on running a boutique hotel on the seafront.

It just happened, really. But whether it was a random act, divine intervention or foolhardy adventure, I still can't say. Perhaps all three.

It was a chain reaction ignited three years earlier that led us to Sri Lanka. I was in Barcelona when John called from Sydney. 'It's all over. The festival's dead,' he croaked down the phone.

His distress was palpable. I'd never heard him express doubt, fear or pain ever, throughout our marriage. The dream of a ground-breaking comedy festival, *The World's Funniest Island,* on Sydney Harbour's Cockatoo Island, was dead. And after only one glorious sun-shiny October weekend of sizzle and pop, when 8,000 people and 200 national and international comedy acts were ferried across Sydney Harbour to this former convict prison and boatbuilding shipyard, now a post-industrial playground. The weekend had been trumpeted as a success, ensuring, or so we thought, that it would become an annual event on Sydney's entertainment calendar.

'The sponsor pulled out, ticket sales were down, and the board pulled the plug. Six weeks out from showtime. It's dead. Terminal.'

On my balcony in Barcelona, looking out over the famous Las Ramblas boulevard at the ornately costumed 'living statues', John's pain pierced me from half a globe away, inducing my own panic.

'I'm coming straight home. Just hang in there. I love you. We'll get through this.'

The festival had been his plan for our future. A yearly event that would set us up. Now he had nothing. No payout and the festival had lots of debts.

My stomach heaved as I felt a wave of resentment wash over me. Right now was supposed to be my kickback time, my days of wine and roses.

Three months earlier, after 17 years working as a production executive in ABC Television Documentaries, I happily accepted a redundancy package to piss off quietly. *Good timing*, I thought to myself back then.

While it was stimulating and rewarding to work with many of the country's cleverest filmmakers, it was also stressful, very stressful, to get it right, as the stakes and network expectations were high. I'd had enough of waking up every night at 3am writing emails in my mind, lying in the dark, unable to get back to sleep, and thinking it was normal.

With television behind me, I catapulted myself into the future by taking off to meet our daughter, Lola, who was studying at a university in Spain. I was relishing living in Barcelona when John called me, leaving me to think...

Hmmm ... reinvention gets harder as you get older.

* * *

John was morose and drowning in angst the night I returned to Australia. The full moon hung half rubbed out by smudges of charcoal clouds; its lack of definition seemed to emphasise the high rotation question in my mind, *where do we go from here?*

Success came early to John. At age 30, he was the impresario of the legendary Last Laugh Theatre Restaurant in inner city Melbourne, which in the late 1970s became the engine room of the 1980s Aussie TV comedy boom. He always spotted the next big somebody before anyone else and his was the loudest laugh at the back of the room.

He spearheaded the first comedy festival in Melbourne and went on to create numerous successful pop-up entertainment events like Red Square, a nightclub constructed out of sea containers for the Adelaide Festival. He created the internationally successful show *Tapdogs,* brought international groups like *Stomp* to Australia for the first time, conceived and produced the Big Laugh Comedy Festival in Parramatta and reformed The Goodies for a national and international tour.

John and I met in a crowded Melbourne nightclub next to John's theatre restaurant, The Last Laugh, listening to the band Mental As Anything's *If You Leave Me, Can I Come Too.*

As a producer I was entertaining a testosterone-driven ABC camera crew on assignment with me for the program '4 Corners' when I spotted John and leant across, asking two questions: do you know where you can get a drink after this place closes, and, what's your name?

John was at the height of his success and notoriety as co-owner of the Laugh so was taken aback that I didn't know who he was. He took great delight for years and years afterwards telling all and everyone that his right-hand producer, Tory McBride, leant across from his other side saying, 'I think she's looking for a root.'

This, of course, ensued, leading me to lose my bra and miss my very early morning plane to Sydney to meet up with a by-then incandescently furious reporter, Kerry O'Brien.

And so I discovered it wasn't hard for things to get messy and out of control while having a huge amount of fun with John Pinder. A calamitous start to a passionate meeting of souls that endured 30 years of rollicking adventures.

On our best days we would tell each other how lucky we were to have met each other because we shared not just a deep love, but also had a shared view of the world and a commitment to a common aesthetic. The defining sign for John that we were soul mates was that we both owned and treasured the book *Bizarre*, an extraordinary compilation by Barry Humphries published in 1965.

John was extremely gregarious, fearless and funny. Very funny, finding the laugh in everything. Without having to try we were always in sync. Even when we argued. Curiously my mother liked to remind me, 'You're so lucky to have met each other because you're both such difficult people.'

I never understood what she meant by this so didn't ask.

* * *

Now failure cut him deeply and because of our enduring connection his flat refusal to talk made me mad. He would not, could not, talk about how he felt and remained locked off, monosyllabic, unable to be reached. Intimacy was failing us. 'John, what are you thinking? Tell me, pleeease. I need to know.'

'Like shit,' he snapped.' I stood up from our table, collected the dinner plates and headed to the kitchen. I was lost for words.

The following day, over breakfast, John sat hunched up over his newspaper. Nothing had changed. I tried to coax an idea out of him; what now? What could our future be?

'Buggered if I know,' he responded flatly.

John stared at his newspaper.

I pushed on. 'We could live in Barcelona for a few months? You said how much you liked it.'

John had visited me there on his way home from the Edinburgh Fringe Festival.

'What do you think? You'd be closer to the Edinburgh Festival—you could take shows there from Australia, maybe cook up something in Spain? I could do some freelance pieces. We could live a bit, do something new?'

John stayed silent.

Sitting in our local cafe overlooking Bondi Beach, I watched a lone sailboat move across the bay in line with the horizon. Slowly, purposefully, being blown by the wind.

'We could be that boat out there, floating free. We've got the money to do it. It's not to say you can't get things off the ground here, but it will take time. Living in Barcelona could be the reset we both need.'

'Mmmmm...' John lifted his head from the newspaper.

His eyes showed a glimmer that I hadn't seen in a while. I took it as a yes. I found a rental agency to manage our house; we packed all the precious stuff into our garage and bought open return tickets to Spain. Lola was excited that we would reunite on the other side of the world. We planned to go to Barcelona, then perhaps to Istanbul, and definitely to the Jaipur Writers' Festival in India.

We were on the road again.

Once we left Australia, John's exuberance slowly returned. He was less inclined to fret about the past or the future and more susceptible to living in the moment. One morning, John looked up from his computer, 'We've got an invitation from an old showbiz mate of mine to come and celebrate New Year's Eve at his hotel in Sri Lanka. He says it's right on a surf beach.'

'Perfect. Let's go.'

We left falling Christmas snow in Istanbul, flying straight into Colombo's fierce tropical heat. Heading for the Surfside

Hotel in Hikkaduwa, on the southwest corner of Sri Lanka, we never imagined that we'd be back managing this rather dilapidated beachside paradise nine months later.

The owner was an English producer, a spider-limbed surfer enthusiast named Nick. For over 25 years, he and John had met at the annual Edinburgh Fringe Festival, scouting for cabaret and comedy talent for their respective clubs.

From touchdown, this ancient island seduced us as we explored it over three enthralling weeks. First, our village Hikkaduwa and nearby Galle, then embarking on an arduous potholed road trip of Sri Lanka's wildly fecund landscape and history. We'd already travelled extensively throughout Asia, Europe and the Americas, but Sri Lanka was the most fascinating place we'd visited.

It had everything. Ruins of fifth and eleventh-century ancient cities that still show traces of remarkable architectural innovation, a rich history as a global trading destination, and a complex, magnetic present as the country steadied itself after three decades of civil war.

First stop was Dambulla, a scruffy, dusty town in the middle of Sri Lanka's Cultural Triangle, north of the old capital Kandy. We wanted to see the renowned Buddha-filled cave temples. These cave temples are a long hot climb up a road high above the garish neon lights of Dambulla's main Buddhist temple. Behind a kitsch verandah facade lies five breathtakingly beautiful small caves containing more than 150 statues and images of the Buddha. Some figures, like the exquisite 14-metre reclining Buddha, are carved directly out of the rock walls; others were installed over the 2,300 years the caves had been a sacred pilgrimage site.

'These caves are the spiritual centre for Buddhism in Sri Lanka. This place is the soul of our country,' a monk told us in a low, soft voice.

In this whole area, maybe 80 cave temples have been found. But only these five were open to tourists because they had been restored.

One statue was freshly painted and looked somewhat out of place behind a new wooden railing. Temple etiquette is to dress respectably in the presence of the Buddha, and good manners demand that nobody turns their back on the Buddha.

The monk explained that a German girl in shorts and a bikini top leapt up into the arms of the Buddha while her boyfriend snapped happy holiday pictures. The monks were horrified, and determined that a cleansing coat of paint and some security rails would restore the statue to bliss.

On our way down the hill, amused and appalled by the tale of the fräulein's faux pas, darkness fell, and the otherwise utterly uninteresting Dambulla main street sparkled with deliciously tacky festoon lighting.

The carnival was in town.

'Sujith, why all these lights?' John asked our driver, his showbiz antennae twitching. 'Ahh, lights for carnival. But not a place tourists like. Music too loud. Foreigners don't go. Only Sri Lankans,' he answers evasively.

'Perfect,' said John.

'We are going. Now.'

'You will be the only foreigners there.'

It's clear he wants to go but is hoping his tourist passengers will return to their boring hotel and bed first.

Chapter 3

WALL OF DEATH

A mad fairyland of lights beckon. John's lifelong passion for circuses and sideshows, which has taken him across Australia, New Zealand, the USA, Europe, and parts of India, is about to go Sri Lankan.

The spruiking is familiar to John, although it's all in Sinhalese. The Wall of Death spectacle is immediately recognisable to him, though even more ramshackle and dangerous than the Occupational Health and Safety-free examples he recalls from his New Zealand childhood.

The Wall of Death is a classic fairground attraction – a huge barrel, perhaps 10 metres in diameter and 10 metres high. Ladders go to the top attached to the outside of the barrel, and the audience stands on a narrow outside platform looking down into the arena. Motorcycle stunt riders zoom around inside the walls doing tricks like 'Look, Mum, no hands'. John claimed that Mexicans specialised in this act.

Standing in front of the spectacular exterior of Dambulla's Wall of Death, John's eyes lit up as he recounted a story about a time that he filmed a gag inside a wall of death with a bunch of Mexican stunt riders zooming around him, 'I stood, scared witless, inside it. I'd replaced the glamorous assistant.'

I was and still am incredulous. John is a big man, a very big man, and at size XXL, 10 sizes larger than any beautiful pint-sized assistant.

'I was terrified that I might get whacked by a stray helmet or a handlebar in a tiny miscalculation, ending up with me being reincarnated as a monkey,' under whose sign John was born according to the Chinese zodiac. He survived to tell me the story but never attempted to enter the Wall of Death again.

At the Dambulla Wall of Death, the laconic stunt team sat out front with a couple of antique motorcycles, a three-wheeler tuk-tuk with the roof removed, and a bicycle. No safety gear, no helmets. The team wore street clothes and sandals.

We paid our 30 rupees each and climbed the rickety ladder, up 10 metres and past the logs wedged against the wall's timber boards held together with cables. Everything was wobbling even with the stunt vehicles still stationary out the front.

Around 20 of us stood on a tiny platform, peering over the edge of the barrel down into the dark. A small trap door opened, letting in a shaft of light. Two floodlights swung on bare wires tied to the centre pole that held up the tattered canvas roof. The platform we were standing on moved as we clambered around. In front-row position were two young monks in saffron robes leaning over the arena eagerly.

'At least they get to be reincarnated if this thing falls over and we all die,' John quipped.

The crackle of unsilenced exhausts is the overture for the main event. This bit is all showbiz. The noise is deafening. Into the arena roars the fleet. The trapdoor is closed. The white floodlights, swinging crazily on the bare wires, switch on, and the girl driving the tuk-tuk takes to the wall. Zooming around the sloped lower ramp, she builds up speed and then whips up the wall. The whole structure shakes and sways wildly. The tuk-tuk zooms up the wall, circling a metre from the top onto the red safety line and threatening to fly right out onto us.

We reel back and I realise there is only a loose rope between us and the ground ten metres below. Exhaust fumes engulf us. The scare factor is off the Richter scale.

I'm terrified. My stomach knots into the tightest of balls, fighting off a panic attack; 'We're gonna die!'

John is entranced

Ten times around the wall. A perfunctory victory wave and the motor cuts. The tuk-tuk coasts down the wall in one silent circuit and stops.

The boys on the bikes fire up. Again the noise is deafening. First one up, then two; looping around in opposite directions. Higher and higher up the wall they go, passing a grubby red scarf from one to the other. The stink of fuel is overwhelming. Again the motors cut simultaneously, and the bikes seem to float on the wall back to the ground.

Cool beyond belief, the riders kickstand the bikes, sit down against the centre pole and ignore us all.

John explains that riding the Wall of Death is easy.

'You need to get up to speed for momentum, and gravity will kick in. Then it's like riding on a straight highway. The fear is all in the structure's noise, creaking, and movement.'

John judges the final guy on the pushbike as a bit of a letdown. Hard work, yes, he says. But the silence and lack of shaking in the walls mean the thrill isn't there.

'It should have been the middle act with a comedy spin! But, hey, that's showbiz,' he says. Always thinking ahead, looking for ways to up the excitement. If we only knew what was to come.

By the time we hit the ground, the Wall of Death Team is selling tickets to the next show, smoking cigarettes and only vaguely interested in the two whacky white tourists praising their daring feats.

We skip the rides and miss the last performance of the other big sideshow... a couple act, where he drives a tractor over her, and then she drives a tractor over him. The handpainted banners showing these feats on the outside of their tent are fabulous.

For John, the Dambulla Cave Temples and the Wall of Death remained the twin highlights of our road trip around the Cultural Triangle. They beat hands down the magnificent ancient capitals – the fifth-century rock citadel, Sigiriya, the eleventh-century Polonnaruwa – and the Kandy Buddhist Temple that houses the Buddha's tooth relic. Dambulla convinced John that Sri Lanka was a place for him. His equilibrium returned, and he no longer fretted about the future, while the warm, cinnamon-scented air back in Hikkaduwa managed to reignite some lost heat between us.

With its small palm-thatched beach bars selling happy-hour cocktails, Hikkaduwa reminded us of Bali's Kuta Beach forty years ago, before mass development destroyed its funky vibe. We gazed at vividly painted sunsets while watching handsome Sri Lankan beach boys pledge undying holiday love to women tourists of all ages, hoping to secure an exit visa.

As we relaxed in the Surfside hotel we couldn't help but notice the dynamic between the local hotel manager, Nalinda, and nattily dressed Stewart, a former British Airways first-class purser turned DJ that Nick had brought in on some vague deal to spruce up the hotel's profile and get more customers. It wasn't good.

As the owner, Nick was worried the hotel didn't have broad appeal despite its picture-perfect location, right on a famous surf break, with many rooms empty during the peak holiday season. The only online reviews mentioned dirty sheets and a general lack of cleanliness.

With surfboards piled up at the entrance, the whole vibe of the hotel was a shabby, eccentric surfers' hang. On Nick's instruction, Stewart tried implementing small cosmetic changes like buying new tablecloths, but the staff either forgot to use them or only half carried out his suggestions.

Sometimes Stewart joined us for a sunset drink, muttering darkly that Nalinda was undermining and turning the staff against him. Nalinda was a plump-featured, lugubrious man in his early forties with soft burnished skin who avoided eye contact with the hotel guests. He regarded the hotel as his family home for his wife, two daughters and pets, rather than a place for guests to come. The overall tone of his staff was indolent and indifferent.

Worse, tensions were rising. The staff were peddling rumours about Stewart. One lurid tale told of him found dead drunk, lying in the garden of a nearby hotel. We found out later that he didn't last long working at the hotel. Nalinda saw to that.

We celebrated with Nick and his girlfriend, Frances, on our last night in Sri Lanka. Her translucent freckled skin and golden hair made her Celtic origins stand out in stark relief in Sri Lanka.

Nick insisted we make a night of it by going to his favourite bar, Ranjith's Beach Hut, a veteran on the Hikkaduwa bar scene for 30 years. Ranjith's was little more than an open-fronted concrete bunker with graffitied walls that paid testimony to its long history as night-time party central.

We scrambled up a wonky set of wooden stairs from the beachfront that were needed because of the post-tsunami erosion that had severely worn away the seafront.

The music on the jukebox cranked up louder and louder as we danced, shouted and laughed up a storm, drinking way too many cocktails; harmless-tasting concoctions made from locally brewed white moonshine that left you minus many valuable brain cells the next day.

We stumbled out of the bar around 4am, heading down the beach back to the hotel, collapsing into a sodden sleep until our alarm buzzed at 8am. Shaking ourselves awake, we joined Nick and Frances for a final breakfast.

All four of us were fuzzy-brained, bleary-eyed, and not saying very much. Out of the blue, Nick blurted out the invitation that was to change our lives.

'I think you should come back and run the place next season. We've told you about the changes we want to make, and you could be just the people to do it. What do you think?'

He sat back in his chair with a mischievous smile playing across his mouth, his pale ice-grey eyes not giving anything away.

Did I hear right? Is he insane? It was such an off-the-wall invitation that I couldn't believe what my ears told me they'd just heard. But what an incredible proposition. John and I looked at each other.

Deadpan, John mumbled, 'Yeah, well, might be interesting; we'll think about it.' We got into the waiting van, waving goodbye to Hikkaduwa.

In the van we couldn't wait to talk about it. 'It could be the most fabulous adventure.'

'Well, let's see if the idea goes anywhere first,' John responded.

I sat in the back of the van, gazing at the now-familiar parade as we hurtled towards the airport. Village dogs on suicide missions to cross the manic road, men on bicycles carrying bunches of giant orange coconuts, a gaggle of ample-fleshed women swathed in saris holding sunset-shaded umbrellas as shields as they walk along the edge of the busy road.

Nick's offer swirled around and around in my mind as many thoughts collided. Maybe it's the recharge that John and I need. A challenge John could meet that would get him over the smouldering misery of his cancelled festival. Taking on such a new challenge and working with John for the first time in our marriage might not be easy but nothing seemed impossible as I watched blurred forests whir by from the van's window.

Serendipity brought us to Sri Lanka. Would it bring us back?

Chapter 4

COME ON OVER

After we'd dropped out of the sky in Sydney with a thumping thud, everything seemed yawningly the same. Nothing had changed in the time we'd been away.

But we had.

People asked us, 'So, how are you enjoying "retirement"? 'We would look at each other, thinking the same thing, 'Retirement from what? Life?'

It made the lure of Nick's offer shimmer and beckon like a jewel.

On a sticky autumn morning with our laptops open, I said what I'd been thinking since Nick had asked us to come.

'Why don't we ask Nick if the offer's for real? Hikkaduwa could be our fantasy come true. Everyone dreams of going to a tropical paradise to run a boutique hotel. Don't they? '

'It could be our last great adventure together before we shuffle off into the twilight zone with all the other grey ghosts. It'd sure get us out of here.' John nailed it in his inimitable way. 'I'll email Nick.'

Back came an answer: 'Yes, the offer's serious; let's talk.'

Skyping Nick from our house in Bondi Beach, we tried to picture gloomy wintery London while experiencing the weird disjoint of time zone difference. Late afternoon in Sydney, we were sipping wine in the warm breeze drifting through the open door while Nick had just finished breakfast on the other side of the world.

John lays it out.

'Nick, we love the idea of running your hotel. But how will it work with Nalinda and his family? He's been running the joint for years, what will he think about us coming in to take over?'

Nick looked and sounded neutral, not giving away much, his pale eyes shielded by small metal-framed glasses.

'Well, you're right, it *is* a sensitive situation, and we all need to work together to make it a smooth transition.' Nick paused for a beat, 'The best thing would be for either or both of you to come to Sri Lanka soon, for a couple of weeks. Spend some time with Nalinda to work it out,' he added vaguely

'I've raised some money from investors to refurbish the place and it needs a proper relaunch, with new branding. You could come for the next tourist season from October to April – then come back for the next season if it all works out.'

'Okay. Dasha and I need to talk about this; I'll get back to you.'

Looking at each other, it was clear we'd already decided. John led off with: 'So, are we ready to become Sri Lanka's least-experienced hotel managers? Are we gonna swap one surf spot for another? And run a hotel into the bargain? Can't see how we can lose, can you?'

'Not really. Can't be that different from running a club or wrangling people making TV programs. Can it?'

What *was* there to lose? Our house would earn more rental money than we would by managing the hotel, and we got to live in and learn about a fascinating culture. Tailor-made for us, as I saw it. A real opportunity to combine travel and adventure with work. And we could jump into it right away. I had one reservation; we'd never worked together.

Looking away from his newspaper John smiled, looking the most relaxed I'd seen him in a very long time. 'I feel great about it. Just as long as you don't turn into a Sybil and I don't become a Basil. I think we have complementary skills that'll make us a great team.'

I could feel John's mood shifting. By a whisker.

'You know, John, if anyone had predicted we would work together in the past, we both would've rolled our eyes and chorused, "I don't think so". What's different now?' I asked.

'We've had 27 long years to figure each other out, and we've sure learnt what buttons not to push. We could have a lot of fun doing this and learn some stuff. But, if it doesn't work out… well, it won't be the end of the world. We'll just come back here.'

I always believed that John's freewheeling, intuitive modus operandi – relying on enthusiasm and constant generation of new ideas – was at odds with my methodological step-by-step procedural approach. So working together was a massive leap of faith on my part.

John's passion for making and selling entertainment achieved for him unexpected fame, notoriety and success in his early twenties. He possessed enormous confidence in his ability to dream a scheme and carry it off. His enthusiasm was infectious, and I always believed he could carry it out until the point when he didn't. Like when we spent months living in New York City while he worked on redesigning, rebuilding and reopening a famous old African-American Harlem nightclub called Smalls Paradise. It never did open, the global financial crisis putting an end to it. We decided to sense-check our plan over dinner with friends, but we only got as far as the pre-dinner drinks before the questions lobbed at us in a volley.

'You've only spent three weeks in Sri Lanka on holiday and now you're going back to manage some run down beach hotel owned by some bloke in the UK? Are you mad?'

'What happens if you get sick, like a heart attack?'
'Do you think this is maybe a delayed mid-life crisis?'
'Isn't there a civil war there?'
'But aren't a lot of Sri Lankans leaving in boats, trying to come to Australia as refugees?'

'No, the war finished in 2009. It's peaceful in Sri Lanka; tourism is starting to boom. And they do have good medical care,' I replied, trying to put a positive spin on the conversation.

Wringing the neck of a champagne bottle, slowly easing the cork out John said: 'Well, maybe all of that's true. But it could be fabulous. You can all come and visit.' The cork popped politely, the champagne cascading into the waiting glasses. John lifted his, 'To Sri Lanka!'

Our friends joined in his toast, clearly not convinced.

None of which deterred us in the slightest.

While John liked to joke that we were Sri Lanka's most inexperienced hotel managers, we had more going for us than we let on. During 40 years as an entertainment producer and showman John had owned and run not just the well-known Last Laugh Theatre Restaurant & Zoo, but restaurants, cafes, nightclubs, festival venues and even a rock'n'roll circus. His bold, exuberant personality loved meeting, greeting, entertaining, and taking people's money at the door. He was the ringmaster.

My career spanned 25 years in factual TV as a current affairs reporter, a documentary producer and, latterly, an ABC Commissioning Editor. It had required collaboration, backing people and creative ideas from inception to broadcast, dealing with tricky personalities, and solving problems on the run. I was more than ready for this new challenge.

Together, we believed we had all the bases covered to be newly minted hoteliers.

John was off to the Edinburgh Festival, and we decided he should stop in Sri Lanka on the way to investigate and see if it was doable.

He needed to find out three basic things: How did Nalinda feel about us coming? How do we go about replacing Nalinda and his wife as the hotel's new managers? What will Nalinda's role be?

But it wasn't just about Nalinda. John needed to find out how Sri Lankans felt about white Western managers in general and specifically in "our" hotel. Would we be accepted or shunned as reminders of a colonialist past? Were there other white Western managers/owners in our village working successfully with Sri Lankan staff? Did they experience any problems?

He also needed to work through with Nick how the influx of investor monies would be allocated. The bottom line – how much money was there?

Within 36 hours of arriving in Hikkaduwa, John called me. 'The Nalinda relationship is more complicated than we thought. He's flip-flopping about everything. As you can imagine, he and his wife have a raft of complex issues in the community about their status that they need to resolve.'

'Well, if he wants us to come and manage the hotel, Nick needs to resolve things with Nalinda. Before we get there,' I said in the most definite tone I could.

'Agree. Also I saw our two rooms today, they need major renovation, carpentry, painting and furnishing before we arrive. There's money in the budget to do it, but I'm not sure they'll get it done on time. It also looks like Nalinda and his family may or may not move out before we get here. I'm pushing as hard as I can.'

I have to admit, this phone call rattled me. It didn't sound straightforward.

While Nick wanted change to happen and us to be its agents, what did Nalinda want? Nick had bought him a block of land to build his own house and arranged temporary accommodation, *but will this be enough to placate Nalinda*, I wondered.

John stayed two weeks in Sri Lanka. We skyped most days (when the unstable internet connection allowed), exploring our readiness to take on the hotel: 'You know, Dasha, I believe we can run with this. Together. What are you thinking?'

'Well, I think we can.'

I could have added that some people would say that familiarity breeds complacency. And while that's true, I prefer to think we'd arrived at a deep acceptance of each other. Warts and all, sliding into a groove of close, amused companionship when we found the time to be together.

We'd tamed our volatile relationship after being held captive to the daily pressures on our lives. There were money problems from John's business ventures, coupled with the stresses of my job in the ambition-driven world of TV, and the perils of raising an adolescent daughter where every boundary imposed became social suffocation.

On top of that there were my health problems after I suffered a series of ischemic stroke attacks at age 50. Then we lost our house in the Pittwater National Park 1994 bushfires. A fireball took it out and reduced it to smouldering ashes in 10 minutes, leaving me knee-deep the next day in the debris, howling like a banshee. All these things add up to couples like us reaching a breaking point, asking, 'Really? Is this all there is? Is this worth it? What the hell are we doing this for?' We climbed back down from this game of brinkmanship a couple of times during our marriage.

Some days later, another phone call from John, 'Looks like we've got a final position on the hotel now. Are you ready for this? Because it's on. I will meet with Nick in Edinburgh to finalise our contract.'

'Oh yeah, I'm ready as long as you believe it's doable for us.'

In a glorious moment of serendipity, a friend asked me to fill in for a month as a stand-in manager at her eight-room boutique Bondi Beach Hotel. All the stars aligned. I learnt the intricacies of folding the perfect hospital bed corner, online booking systems and how to create a thriving holiday environment while nodding politely and appeasing guests suffering the 'princess with a pea under the mattress' syndrome.

And so it was decided, just like that. John and I were to be hoteliers in Sri Lanka. We landed in Colombo three months later.

Chapter 5

ARRIVAL

Arriving alone and bedraggled at Colombo Bandaranaike airport, I was leaden-limbed from sleeping origami-style from Barcelona.

John's steady-as-a-rock persona had always been my reality check in unknown situations, but this time, his work commitments meant he flew into Sri Lanka on a different airline from another country. Something that seemed so perfectly normal at the time we booked our tickets had left me feeling totally out of whack when I arrived.

A sense of déjà vu hit me as I queued for a tourist visa, wrapped in the familiar blanket of frangipani-scented humid heat, a heat that smothers you like a wet towel, makes your brain soggy and forces you into slow motion.

Ahhhh, I'm back in Sri Lanka ... no rush here. The dizziness and stomach churning subsided. A momentary panic passed.

Outside the airport, Sujith's familiar wide smile, studded with gleaming pearl teeth, welcomed me as he swung my bags with his lithe limbs into our hotel's eight-seat van. 'Madame Dasha, you come back to Sri Lanka. I very happy to see you.' Sujith was our hotel's driver, whom we got to know when we stayed on holiday nine months earlier. We embraced awkwardly in the European style, as I am still unclear about the proper etiquette between me, the new Anglo-woman hotel manager, and him as a Sri Lankan man. I remember that public displays of affection between Sri Lankans of the opposite sex are non-existent. And they are considered inappropriate.

Hmmm – this will be a steep learning curve – finding the balance between the Sri Lankan and my way. And it's all going to be pretty much on the fly, telegraphed my crowded mind. Expat men look to have much smoother social interactions than western women in Sri Lanka. Perhaps because it's a male-dominated society, expat men seem to get the rules of the game instinctively, while Sri Lankan mores appeared to me to prescribe women's behaviour. Thoughts were continually running in my mind like a news strapline on the bottom of a TV screen.

There's going to be some challenges for this Aussie woman. One who is used to doing things my way and rarely acquiesces to something I don't agree with.

In the chaos of the crazy, exhaust-belching, horn-honking, suicidal Colombo traffic, we passed a ninja-like driver weaving a ubiquitous tuk-tuk through the traffic. I laughed out loud reading the back of its roof canopy, in proud capitals:

TRUE LOVES COME ONCE IN A LIFETIME.

I was back in the funny, exotic, complex, tropical 'paradise' of Sri Lanka.

John knocked on my Galle Face Hotel room door some hours later, and we fell into each other's arms, collapsing onto the bed together, luxuriating in the warmth of each other's bodies. It was the mystique of Sri Lanka at work, because we hadn't felt this heat between us in quite some time. Perhaps it was this memory of the sensuous heat between us amidst lush tropical surroundings that fuelled our desire to return. Later, we lapped up the famous hotel splendour, sitting on the renowned chequerboard patio in front of the sea, clinking our cocktail glasses, 'To you, to us'. We toasted our newly-minted life as the island's least practised hoteliers.

He looked around the manicured lawn edging the patio, 'It sure beats the shit out of what they call "retirement", I feel the best, the happiest I've been in years. I've got such a good feeling about all this, Dasha.' Our hands came together across the small table.

'I think it's auspicious that we're launching our paradise adventure in *this* hotel. It's as if some of it's giving us a hotelier's blessing.'

The Galle Face Hotel is one of those remnants of the British Raj that makes British tourists think they still rule the world. Reputedly the oldest hotel east of Suez, it opened in 1864, and the ghosts of kings, queens, generals, movie stars and writers are immortalised in an eccentric collection of photos, plaques and busts in the foyer that preempts the star memorabilia of any Hard Rock Cafés.

When he was a guest, Noel Coward premiered his satirical song about what was then known as Ceylon, 'Mad Dogs and Englishmen', on the hotel's grand piano. One 19-year-old off-duty British Navy sailor stationed there at the outbreak of WWII bought himself a small English car for about five hundred rupees to go touring. Now remembered as the Duke of Edinburgh, his lovingly restored 1935 Standard Nine is an eccentric souvenir of his visit, proudly on display in the foyer.

Long-time Sri Lankan resident Arthur C. Clarke completed the final chapters of *2001: A Space Odyssey* there, calling the Galle Face 'Tranquillity Base'. His flattery earned him a large bronze bust in the foyer.

The hotel's recent history had its share of infamy, with the most rambunctious of all Sri Lankan New Year's Eves in 2002. Five hundred of Colombo's beautiful people partied in the New Year under the stars. One of them, a Sri Lankan government minister's son, spotted his ex-girlfriend dancing with another man. He became enraged, ordering his armed private security to fire pistol shots in the air, scattering everyone.

Hotel staff told us that the discharge of lethal weapons in five-star hotels was not unusual during this epoch of civil war.

Later that afternoon, Kottarapattu Chattu Kuttan, the legendary, 90-year-old doorman, in his gold-brocaded white jacket with his white handlebar moustache, summoned a car to drive us to our new life at Surfside Hotel in Hikkaduwa. Driving through Colombo, a giant billboard advertising the Amana Bank struck me as promising: 'Your bank believes ethics and social responsibility take priority over profits.'

'Well, that'd be a first. We should send a photo of that to our bank in Sydney.' We swung onto the recently completed Chinese-funded tollway hurtling south. I was bursting with excitement and jitters.

'I know what that phrase feels like, "with my heart in my mouth", because that's where it is. It's thumping.'

John squeezed my hand but said nothing as he gazed out the window.

After sunset, we pulled off the main road through Surfside Hotel's open front gates to stop on the gravel drive. Some familiar faces greeted us effusively as we looked at our new home, a modest, British-style white bungalow building with a red-tiled roof, surrounded by an ad hoc tropical garden.

Jayantha the housekeeper, a sombre-looking civil war veteran, remembered us from our previous visit. 'Welcome back, Mr John and Madame Dasha. We very happy you come back to Hikkaduwa.'

Behind him stood Latith, the boyish, small-framed waiter from our previous trip, shyly greeting us while taking our bags into the hotel. John and I walked side by side down the corridor towards the beachfront – it all looked much shabbier and dingier than I remembered from nine months earlier.

Discoloured, dust-encrusted coir matting ran from the front door down the long 20-metre central corridor, with most of the floor-recessed light bulbs blown. The once-white walls flecked with scuff marks. As we walked, without speaking or looking at each other, I felt John's heart sinking fast, just as mine was.

'Maybe we're just dispirited from travel exhaustion.'

We stood in the courtyard, facing the beach with our bags at our feet. John and I slowly turned, facing each other with that 'whoa, what have we gotten ourselves into here' look. Then, with just a glance, we silently resolved that everything could wait until tomorrow. At least we'd arrived. But the man we were to replace wasn't there.

'Strange, don't you think, John, that Nalinda's not here to welcome us?'

'I'm sure we'll see him tomorrow. Right now, I want to check out our room.'

While John slept log-like, I tossed and turned, waking up at dawn feeling discombobulated. Instinctively, I wanted to plunge myself into the champagne-like fizzing surf in front of the hotel to soothe and wash away my mind's jangles.

Wrapping a sarong over my swimsuit, I walked through the courtyard towards the beach, passing the empty open-sided restaurant pavilion on my right side, with its 10 forlorn tables waiting for customers. Then, smack in front of me, the world-famous Hikkaduwa surf break. Heaven.

White-crested waves pounded the shoreline only 15 metres from where I stood, on top of a sandy embankment that marked the hotel's borderline from the beach. The softest peach-coloured light caressed the pale grey silk sea and the sky's feathery clouds. Scrambling over a pile of sandbags shoring up the eroded hotel beachfront, I stepped straight into the finest pale golden sand. I stood gazing to my left at a stunning unbroken shoreline, stretching for several kilometres.

I walked into the waves and plunged under them. Bliss.

One of my most sensual pleasures is diving headfirst into the boundless aquamarine blue sea; untameable, unpredictable and ungovernable. As islanders, Australians claim to have swimming in their DNA, and swimming has always been my way of sustaining an equilibrium between a sometimes contrary mind and a recalcitrant body.

Perhaps my comfort in the water comes from some primordial impulse, knowing that the ocean is a life force of its own, not to be feared but to be mastered with knowledge and respect. When I'm submerged, silently stroking through the water, it becomes a meditation as the focus switches to the rhythm of my arm strokes, the kicking of my legs and then the slow intake of breath propelling me forward.

The tingling of the water on my skin is intensely pleasurable; it gives rise to euphoric random thoughts and memories. As a child growing up in a landlocked suburban house in Melbourne, mermaids held sway over my fantasy world. The fish-to-man/woman notion of evolution was entirely believable to me.

Maybe it all began in the late 1950s, when my father threw me into the Gold Coast's Chevron Hotel swimming pool in a sink-or-swim approach to swimming lessons. I swam and haven't stopped. My childhood's sea siren myths and folktales float through my spirit world when I swim. No surprise that I've spent the last 40 years, on and off, living at and being inspired by the sea, physically needing to see the water, walk by it, or swim in it every day.

This beach landscape was just as I remembered it – a postcard tropical paradise with swaying palm trees fringing the golden sandy beach. The wooden sandwich board stuck in the sand next door advertised surfboard hire, and surf lessons in Russian and English; a reminder that this funky paradise is available to all tourists with a wallet.

***

Since former US champion Rusty Miller surfed Sri Lanka in 1965 (describing the island as a Shangri-La for surfers) Hikkaduwa has been on the world map; famed for its user-friendly surf, breaking over flat coral reefs and sandy points.

Sri Lanka is unique for such a tiny island; only 440 kilometres in length and 220 kilometres wide. Climatically it's split in two, with the east and west of the island experiencing different monsoon seasons. This means that Hikkaduwa, in the southwest, is a surfer's paradise from October through to May with the monsoon hitting it from June until September.

Arugam Bay, on the island's east side, is famed for its surf breaks from April through to October, with its monsoon season running from November through to March. This guarantees that the island is a surfer's Shangri-La all year round.

I walked along the shorefront, watching a few dawn surfers catching some laid-back waves while a few bikinied bodies bobbed in the warm turquoise sea. Further along the shoreline, 20 or so village men of all ages hauled a long, thin, red wooden fishing boat up onto the beach after the night's expedition. With the catamaran firmly wedged in the wet sand, they heaved and pulled a heavy green fishing net filled with the night's catch destined for the nearby Dodanduwa fish market. Standing knee-deep in the waves, their legs at a forty five-degree angle, with their feet planted in the wet sand, they strained every sinewy muscle taut in their bodies, with jaws clenched. Strong, lean men doing tough work.

When I turned back to walk in the other direction past our hotel, I noticed the beach erosion had worsened since we were there. The sea comes up to the sea walls of some of the guesthouses and bars down the beach from us. Erosion of the coral reefs through fishing, quarrying for lime and harvesting tourist souvenirs has caused the visible tidal change.

I walked back through a sleeping hotel to our front gate and was shocked at how narrow the strip of land was between the front entrance on the main road and the sea – only the width of the hotel and the beach, approximately 60 metres in total. I had remembered this distance as much broader. Now it doesn't make me feel too comfortable, because this area on the south coast was severely affected by the 2004 tsunami.

I remembered a conversation I had on our first visit to Hikkaduwa with a small bar owner in the village, who told me that a regulation had been introduced after the tsunami that all buildings had to be rebuilt 100 metres back from the beach. What that meant was that the hotels would have to be off the beach, across the crazy main road out front, over on the jungle side near the railway line.

'All the hotel owners got together, saying, "No good, we'll lose business. Tourists come just for the surf. They won't stay on the jungle side of Galle Road. They only want to be beach-side".' He rolled his eyes and shrugged his shoulders. 'What to do?' he asks.

This phrase, 'what to do', was a mantra we came to hear often.

Post-tsunami development in Hikkaduwa was rampant, unchecked and unregulated. All these properties were crammed up to the roadside cheek by jowl like a sideshow alley.

The two-lane Galle Road out the front of the hotel runs to Colombo. It is a shrieking cacophony of beeping horns, loudspeakers blaring political slogans, four-wheel drives, three-wheeler tuk-tuks, motorcycles and buses – often four vehicles abreast in the two lanes in a crazy dodgem car race with no finish.

One government bus company and several private ones would race each other at breakneck speeds to pick up passengers at the designated bus stops. Sometimes it was a death-defying experience riding in a tuk-tuk; I learnt to close my eyes as the buses hurtled by. Seatbelts are not an optional extra.

On either side of the road, alongside and opposite our hotel, there were dozens of cheap clothing shops, surfboard hire stores, jewellery galleries and hole-in-the-wall kiosks selling Sri Lankan pancakes called roti. One menu item read like a relic of the halcyon, marijuana-fuelled 1960s and 70s – a roti filled with chocolate and banana. The kiosk owner told me the hippies on the overland Asia to Europe travellers' trail introduced this delicacy and it has remained a firm favourite for the last 50 years.

The village is just as I remembered, and the beach just as beautiful, just as seductive.

Chapter 6

NALINDA

Mid-morning, Nalinda gingerly emerged into the courtyard from his family's rooms in the hotel. His plump-featured bronzed face smiling ever so faintly. But his expression was wary, with his body rigid, wearing his worn, dark cap over his eyes and balding head, neatly pressed jeans and a black polo shirt with the slogan 'THE X MAN' discreetly embroidered on the back of his neck and around his shirt sleeve.

'Hello,' he greeted us, 'You've arrived.'

His refusal to make eye contact and reticent expression made it clear he wasn't ecstatic to see us. John tried to bridge this awkwardness by saying, 'Nalinda, this is my wife, Dasha.'

'Yes,' he said, looking at the ground. At 190-centimetres tall, weighing over a hundred kilos and wearing his large square-framed bright yellow glasses, John towered over Nalinda in bulk, height and presence.

Nalinda had worked at the Surfside Hotel as a waiter when Nick came to stay as a guest on a surfing safari from the UK in the early 2000s. The hotel was for sale. Nick, urged on by Nalinda, bought the business with an English friend to create a haven for artists. Nalinda was installed as the new hotel manager, going on to get married, bring his bride home, and have two children. They all had the run of this down-at-heel hotel. It was their home, and they rented out rooms to passing tourists. With the TV blaring as you walked in the front door, hotel reviews had criticised the lack of customer service, and few people came.

I remembered John's earlier phone call, from Sri Lanka, warning me that Nalinda and his family might not leave the hotel. When we arrived, Nick emailed a new schedule indicating that Nalinda and his family would move out in a few weeks. But he didn't nominate a date.

Three days after our arrival, Nalinda was testy and terse, not wanting to share any decision-making and curtly avoiding any discussion. So much to do, and only eight weeks before the first booked guests of the season were to arrive. We couldn't have him offside.

'Nalinda, don't you think we should buy the kitchen equipment we discussed this week? That way, we know what we have. We can store it all in one of the empty rooms?' Nalinda looked at me, eyes blazing, his nostrils flaring as he wheeled away and took off. Without a word.

Minutes later, John barrelled out of the hallway, looking spooked while picking his way across the hotel courtyard, which was littered with tools, paint cans and renovation debris.

'Dasha, what did you say to Nalinda? He's furious. He's stormed off.'

'All I said was that we should go ahead and buy the kitchen equipment. It set him off. Maybe he doesn't like having to deal with a woman. Best, I think, if you deal with him and you do all the talking.'

'Probably a good idea.' He walked off back into the hotel.

While we never knew what Nalinda understood our role in the hotel was to be, we did know that the bond between Nick and Nalinda was ironclad; forged forever when the devastating tsunami hit Sri Lanka on 26 December 2004, killing a total of

32,000 people, destroying 70,000 homes and leaving the surrounding southern coastline looking like a lunar wasteland.

We were told that at Surfside Hotel, it was the old gardener who first set off the alarm about the coming tsunami. He told Nalinda early on that fateful Boxing Day morning that there was something weird going on that he'd never seen before. The tide had pulled offshore by five hundred metres, creating an eerie sand flatland right in front of the hotel.

The first wave hit at 9.30 am. Nalinda and Nick scrambled to get everyone out of the fully-booked hotel. Adults and children ran inland as fast as water rushed through the hotel, rising rapidly over two metres in the central corridor. Everyone escaped safely in only the clothes they were wearing. The rocky outcrop in front of the hotel that created the famous surf break significantly reduced the tsunami's full force.

John and I came to learn that the devastation of the tsunami still cast a black shadow everywhere. Not just throughout our village of Hikkaduwa, but in the surrounding towns of Kahawa, Telwatte, Kalupe and Dodanduwa.

Everyone you meet has a story either of heartbreaking disaster or miraculous escape. I spotted a tiny tsunami museum from a tuk-tuk one day early on in our time in Hikkaduwa, just a couple of kilometres up the road. Set up in the shell of a house destroyed by the tsunami, the museum was owned and run by a woman with the saddest of stories.

When the wall of water smashed the coast, her husband drowned, her baby washed out of her arms, and she only survived by running two kilometres inland. Now, with just a rough corrugated roof over the battered walls and earthen floors, there were many graphic photos, harrowing children's drawings, and handwritten signs trying to make sense of this apocalyptic event.

The drawings showed rushing water with up-ended legs and people holding babies above their heads; another was of a derailed train with up-ended carriages. The museum was near the railway tracks where the second wave obliterated over 1200 people as they tried to escape on a train to Colombo.

John and I went there together. Raw pain leeched off the walls as we stand in front of a sign that reads:

> A dead child can never laugh again, whatever its race.
> A dead parent can never keep its family, whatever
> its religion.
> A lost generation can never be retrieved.

A colossal sob rose in my throat. John became very, very quiet. Another sign tries to find the reason for the impossible:

> All things are impermanent.
> This example is Lord Buddha's sermon.

John turned to leave, 'It's too much.' Further down the road, towards our hotel, a 30-metre-tall beatific sandstone Buddha, gifted by the Japanese government, gazes out to sea over a peaceful pool guarded by four marble lions. It commemorates all the Sri Lankans whose lives got wiped out in the tsunami: 2000 of whom were locals from the immediate area.

This statue mourns not only the lives lost but also the many Buddhist viharas (monasteries) and dagobas (stupas) that the tsunami obliterated. The figure is a replica – carved in the style of the Afghani Buddhas of Bamiyan, which were destroyed by the Taliban in 2001. Amplifying the sense of loss.

About 50 metres from the tsunami photo museum set up in 2006, we notice a copycat museum has popped up in recent years.

'Don't you think it's strange there are two tsunami museums so close together? Given they're both showing more or less the same kinds of images?' I ask John.

'Competition for the donation dollar, I guess. Where there's a tourist buck to be made, they're going to go after it. And who can blame them,' shrugging his shoulders.

People still recall the ferocity of that day with such vivid detail, and the shock of its savagery still reverberates. The trauma of the tsunami was intensified when the ceasefire then failed in the decades-long civil war between the Sri Lankan armed forces and the rebel Tamil Tigers in the north. Again the country was submerged into an increasingly vicious civil war that lasted another five years.

There was no time for Sri Lanka to recover from one disaster before being engulfed in another, even more deadly.

While damaged houses in Hikkaduwa were mostly rebuilt over time, shells of houses still stood like toothless smiles on either side of the village – a silent and poignant testimony.

Despite his blood-brother bond with Nalinda, Nick had expressed concern about some poor online reviews the hotel received. We deduced that the businessman in him worried that the hotel suffered from a poor understanding of the changing face of tourism in Sri Lanka. The location is sublime, but the service is dire. Something had to change. Nalinda and his family would need to move out, and other managers move in. Managers that understood western tourist expectations. Us.

But the one complication in this scenario was that Nick needed to keep Nalinda as his fixer and bagman. It was Nalinda who dealt with the bank to deposit the hotel's cash income; it was Nalinda who sorted out the ongoing problems with the power and internet companies and handled the renovations by finding and organising the workers. He was Sinhalese. Local. He knew the community and spoke their language. We were foreigners. And didn't speak the language.

Being the hotel manager had given Nalinda a certain status in the community up until we arrived, commanding respect. We knew he was worried about how his status would be affected if we took over his role.

Finding a solution to this problem seemed to be our biggest challenge.

Chapter 7

THE COUNTDOWN BEGINS

Diving in headfirst, we cleared out all the hoarded stuff stashed around the hotel. Out of the 15 hotel rooms, one was crammed floor to ceiling with broken furniture, bed frames, rotting mattresses, rusted appliances, boxes of empty old bottles and assorted debris. Then we opened the doors of the oversized enclosed garage. Once, it housed the hotel's tuk-tuk. No longer. Now it was packed to bursting point with unused and unusable paraphernalia including a six-arm espresso machine, broken in transit from the UK. It had never been used or fixed.

Seven trailer loads of refuse went to the local tip.

Waves of workers – painters, electricians, gardeners and carpenters – started arriving, bringing the hotel alive and into shape.

The continual drain of the civil war created such a lack of resources and money that Sri Lankans don't want to throw anything away, believing all broken things can and will be fixed and reused. While this is sustainably responsible in theory, the to-be-fixed pile mushroomed over the years, and nothing ever was.

In the middle of this chaos, two smooth-skinned, grey-haired men sat on small pieces of fabric on the cement floor leading to the dining pavilion. One bare-chested with a long checked sarong gathered between his knees, the other wearing an impeccably white singlet and ecru-coloured sarong. Each man was armed with just a plastic-handled knife as they wove the long warp and weft strands of new cane into an open weave rattan seat square onto a chair frame. Weaving fast and dexterously, they replaced the broken dining chair seats that languished, locked away.

We'd discovered these weavers by accident. Some days earlier, sitting in the back of a tuk-tuk on the road to Galle, John suddenly leapt in his seat, 'Stop. Stop, Rasika. Pull over. I want to check this place out.' He'd spied an open-fronted hole-in-the-wall furniture shop with newly woven cane furniture displayed on the roadside.

John introduced himself to the owner Adith, an affable, bearded, bare-chested young man wearing perfectly pressed jeans and a designer-copy belt with interlocking Gs. His three wiry-bodied craftsmen, bare-chested, barefooted and wearing traditional sarongs, sat on low wooden stools on the concrete floor, up against bright lime green walls. Weaving their magic, they turned out beautiful chairs, tables, sofas and light shades based often on merely a thumbnail sketch or a photo. It was evident that the talent and skills of these local craftsmen, coupled with cheap labour costs, meant that we could order any furniture we needed for reasonable prices. There was no local IKEA here; artisans made beautiful things on a needs-only basis.

John spotted a spherical, pendant lampshade about forty centimetres in diameter. 'Adith, can you make one of those lampshades, but this wide?'

He stood with his arms outspread like an eagle in flight, showing an enormous wingspan from the left-hand fingertip to the right-hand fingertip of over one and a half metres.

'Yes, yes, can do ... very, very, very big lampshade. But we can do it.'

He seemed nonplussed as to why John would want a lampshade so big. But John saw this large woven cane lampshade as a great design feature in the hotel's front lobby, hanging over the long corridor entrance through to the courtyard. When it was up it did look strikingly stylish. Lit up, it looked like a sea urchin's shell, casting beautiful shadows on the walls and ceiling. Some guests liked it so much they ordered ones exactly like it to take home, challenging the limits of excess airline baggage.

Working with Adith's workshop introduced us to the elasticity of 'Sri Lankan Time'.

There could be no doubt that we were assured of exquisitely executed cane furniture. But when we asked how long it would take to produce any given item, there was always the same standard answer: 'Aaaaahhhhh ... Maybe five days.'

This could sometimes translate into delivering anything up to three weeks later. Or more. After many anxious conversations, we slowly understood that when asked 'how long?' the craftsman gave us the answer he thought we wanted to hear, often bearing no relation to the actual time it would take. With just six weeks to go, it became a mounting freak-out as to whether or not there would be furniture to sit on when the first guests arrived.

Even more daunting than accommodating Sri Lankan time was the hotel's kitchen. When I first stood in its doorway, I felt utterly overwhelmed. There was no usable equipment; rusted cutlery and kitchenware were discarded on an open shelf, beyond salvage. An irreparably broken-down freezer sat off in an alcove. A rising panic engulfed me, causing my head to pound.

Convulsed by the impossibility of what lay ahead, I couldn't utter a single word to John, who was standing outside the kitchen window. I was dumbstruck. Literally.

My panic began to subside like a retreating tide as I remembered that my friend Sophie was arriving in two weeks. I had utter faith in her. Australian chef, cookbook author and friend living in Barcelona, Sophie had decided on a whim that she would come to Sri Lanka. She wanted to learn about Sri Lankan cuisine and offered to help us redesign the hotel's kitchen and devise a modern fusion Sri Lankan/Mediterranean menu.

We had been sitting at a cafe in a shady square in downtown Barcelona on a late summer afternoon, drinking vermouth and eating tapas when John and I told her about our plans to run a surfside Sri Lankan hotel.

Listening intently to our story without saying a word, Sophie suddenly announced, 'Well, I think I should come there. And design the menu. And set up the kitchen!' John and I had looked at each other, the idea exploding like a mushroom cloud in our heads as I said what John was thinking, 'You know what, that's a *great* idea, Sophie. You should definitely come to Sri Lanka.'

And so it was agreed.

The timing worked for Sophie; she wanted a short break from an emotionally volatile chapter in her marriage. As an experienced Asian-food chef, she'd owned a Thai restaurant in Barcelona, and Sri Lanka would provide her with a new culinary adventure, learning a new cuisine.

All the stars seemed aligned as this stroke of serendipity brought us all together to solve the kitchen question.

Chapter 8

FIVE WEEKS TILL SHOWTIME

With five weeks to go before the first guests were booked in and one week to Sophie's arrival, the pressure was building. John and I tell each other we're confident that we're on top of things.

Repeatedly.

Or so I think until the Toots & the Maytals' song, 'Pressure Drop', plays on our boombox one day …

"You gonna feel it …

That you were doing it wrong wrong wrong."

With the countdown on, and the renovation chaos swirling around us, the song keeps reverberating and reverberating. Over and over again in my head. An earworm I can't get rid of.

Together with an earworm thought knocking in my mind: *Maybe we're not as on top of things as we think.*

One morning John was walking down the hotel corridor toward me when I saw that he was walking at quite an angle. Lopsided, bent sideways, with a grimace on his face. 'You okay?' I ask. 'Because you don't look it.'

'My back. It's gone out. Again. It's killing me. It'll be okay if I can find a physio. Don't tell me again to go to the Ayurvedic clinic in the village. Because they don't have a clue how to deal with it.'

A sports physio in Galle came to the hotel; pummelled and pulled him into shape, leaving him walking tall. One problem down, fixed for the moment.

Every day we wrote lashings of lists. To-do lists, to buy lists, to get lists, to find lists, to fix lists, and to hire lists. John wrote weekly to-do lists that I put into a spreadsheet. I loved the feeling of efficiency brought on by creating and looking at this document. 'We are getting somewhere.'

Even if, deep down, I couldn't be sure we were.

John's week five list, of must-have-done-or-fail-to-open, trumpeted:

- Complete sandbagging
- Complete lawn
- Repair and check sunbeds
- Create signage x 2 beachside
- Arrange sign-writer or digital
- Build signage frames
- Repair beach showers
- Purchase and install 10 assorted parafloods
- Clear pots, clean up the garden
- New pot plants for the base of the tree
- Assess large pots for décor
- Resolve broken ground lights
- New cane furniture to be delivered
- Purchase/install new lighting with dimmers
- Menu/drinks blackboards
- Wall fridge in the bar – fix? Replace?
- Paint exterior of the bar, including upper fascia
- Repair interior of the bar
- Repair and gloss finish bar top

- Replace bar bench and under shelving
- Clean bar sink, totally repair/replace tap
- Purchase/install sound system
- Build/install new shelving and bar top as designed
- Assess glassware stock & arrange new glasses as req.
- Repaint entire central hallway through to walkway
- Repaint all downstairs rooms
- Repaint & clean upstairs to room 15
- Install new aircon units in all rooms
- Replace all toilet seats
- Replace all showerheads

Etcetera, etcetera, etcetera. Daunted doesn't even begin to describe my reaction when I read it.

Showtime was bearing down on us. Big time. While the list items got ticked off, we advertised for hotel staff, interviewing 30 people out of the 50 replies from our local newspaper advertisement. From the shortlist, John and I assembled a team we felt proud to work with. All nine men we hired had some previous hospitality experience; most had studied hospitality courses at college.

Only men applied for the jobs we advertised, as we discovered it isn't socially acceptable for young women to work in hotels, except if they are beautiful enough to work at the reception desk and as hostesses in glamorous five-star places. Through this experience of hiring staff, we learn that a woman's sexual virtue is a central tenet of Sinhala Buddhism: the community's concern with women's virginal purity is paramount in the marriage stakes.

But it's not the same for men. They are encouraged to 'sow their wild oats' while young and gain any experience on offer.

I found this double standard confronting; although, when I really thought about it, was it so very different in my own culture where a woman's virtue is questioned and pitted against the latitude afforded men when it comes to louche behaviour.

Interviewing, assessing and hiring staff felt familiar to me.

It called on the same skills I used when putting together a crew for a production: sussing out people's strengths, weaknesses, their ability to work together, on top of their obvious skill sets.

But I did feel uncertain as to whether we could accurately judge character. In such an unfamiliar cultural context, it's very tricky to know if you are on the right track. Body language isn't universal, and cultural mores are so different that it is difficult to read how they affect unspoken behaviours. John and I spent a day poring over the notes we made in the interviews, evaluating each person, and trying to understand how they would work together as a team. All we could rely upon was instinct. An instinct that would prove to be fallible.

Aside from lodging the newspaper advertisements in Sinhala, Nalinda was largely absent from the hiring process by simply not being available. He looked over the applicants' resumes but made no comment and declined to participate in the interviews, saying he was too busy building his own house.

Three of our new team were in the kitchen as a chef, second chef and kitchen hand; three young men were to work as housekeepers maintaining the guests' rooms. Two new waiter/barmen, Wasanta and Vinod, were to alternate between the restaurant and bar, joining forces with Latith, the wispy slow-moving waiter we'd inherited, who slept in the bunk-bed staff room, and was a hotel inclusion as permanent as the furniture. Or so we were told by Nick.

One stocky young man, Oshan, stood out in the interviews because of his experience, good English, charm and quick wit. In his late 20s, he'd worked at McDonald's in Saudi Arabia. Like many young Sri Lankan men, who couldn't find local employment, he could earn much better money working in the UAE. But homesickness brought him back to his family and our hotel as a housekeeper. He proved to be an enterprising and valuable ally. Helpful in letting us know what the staff were thinking and getting information to them that we needed to be precise. We bookmarked him as manager material, so it was devastating when he had to go back to work in Dubai three months later to fulfil a disputed contractual obligation.

We decided to risk hiring handsome, inexperienced eighteen-year-old Suresh as a housekeeper. He was straight out of school, spoke okayish English, and was keen to join us. His peacock-like appearance, with gel-slicked stylish haircut, cool sunglasses tucked into the neck of his perfectly pressed T-shirt, and winning smile proved to be a hit with our guests. He became king of the Facebook sultry selfie, featuring an extensive sunglasses collection. Oshan and Suresh joined Jayantha, the civil war veteran already in his third year working at the hotel as a housekeeper.

We were sure the kitchen gods were smiling down on us when we found chef Adith. He was in his late fifties and knew how to cook a lobster thermidor. Not that we wanted this dish to feature on our menu, but it told us he was experienced beyond the basic curry/rice menus of the local budget hotels. He was a station chef in a five-star hotel in Galle, making him the perfect candidate to work with Sophie to set up our new kitchen and create the modern Sri Lankan fusion menu we wanted to introduce. The deal clincher was his genuine interest in the recipes John showed him in Sophie's published cookbook *My Barcelona Kitchen*. Adith, with his sunny disposition, turned out to be an absolute pearler.

He brought with him his second chef, Ari, who was his son-in-law. They were to be assisted by the grandmotherly Mrs Prema, another non-negotiable staff member we inherited from Nalinda. Her primary role was to cook the all-important daily staff meal and be the dishwasher.

With our team in place, we were ready to go. The one staff position we wanted, but never succeeded in getting, was an independent bookkeeper. The hotel operated on a cash basis with handwritten receipts for the restaurant and bar that relied on the waiters remembering what people had ordered and then writing it down. Dicey. Despite trying to introduce a more professional and accountable system, it never happened. Nalinda remained responsible for tracking expenditure, delivering the cash stored in the hotel's safe to the bank, and was the only one with access to the hotel's bank account.

* * *

In my forays to source hotel wares, I encountered the most enticing eruption of colour when I wandered into the large Colombo emporium, Barefoot.

I was bedazzled by the brilliance of the hues around me, an Aladdin's cave of bedspreads, curtains, hand-loomed fabrics, clothes, antiques, books and homewares. There were gossamer-thin silk sarongs woven in the saturated greens of the rice paddies, striped up against the iridescent blue of the peacock's neck and the indigo of the deep ocean. They shimmered like exotic butterfly wings as they floated from their hangers.

This emporium was the creation of one woman – the renowned, now deceased Barbara Sansoni, who revolutionised colour and design in Sri Lanka. She created a cottage weaving industry in the 1960s, and her team of artists continue to design and manufacture their primary-coloured hand-loomed fabrics for clothes and furnishings under the brand name Barefoot today.

But it wasn't just the quality of the weaving and the brilliance of the colours that impressed me. I wanted to know what sparked Barbara's inspiration and found this quote:

I continue to seek the honesty of making a plain piece of cloth but making it divinely and simply beautiful. Barefoot is about people; it's the story of simplicity. The principle behind the business is to develop lifelong skills and give women employment so they can support themselves.

It is a story that has grown into one of Sri Lanka's more successful export businesses over the last 50 years. Barbara Sansoni's woven, rectilinear, abstract style, with no embellishments or decorations, exhibits the bright palate of Sri Lanka – the orange of the monk's robes, striped against fuchsia pink and blood red. The hand-loomed woven cotton fabrics make the most vivid and beautiful bed covers: I bought six of them to feature in our premium, white-painted, concrete-floored oceanfront rooms.

And even today, as I lie under the brilliant orange, hot pink and red stripes of the bedspread I brought back to Australia, I feel cocooned in a Sri Lankan sunset. The colours rush back memories of tropical intensity and the smell of cinnamon oil.

Barbara wasn't the only Sansoni whose work we displayed in our hotel. Her son Dominic Sansoni, a leading Sri Lankan photographer, agreed that we could showcase 10 of his magnificent photographic prints, selected from his coffee table book *Colour*, a vibrant paean of love to his homeland. We displayed them framed, gallery style, along the white walls of the long entrance corridor and offered them for sale.

We wanted to showcase different artists' work throughout the hotel, fulfilling the promise of the hotel slogan John had come up with:

FINE FOOD, FINE ART, FINE SURF

Despite the pressure we were under building to showtime, this was when John was at his happiest in Sri Lanka – designing the 'look' of the hotel and marketing materials. The website, the welcome folders for the rooms, the menu folders, the large street signs to lure patrons in, and a new illuminated sign for the front gate advertising the hotel. Rebranding the hotel and creating its new look became his passion.

Designing venues and managing hospitality logistics was the thing John was very good at, creating entertainment spaces for people's carousing. Like the pop-up nightclub venue, Red Square, he created from sea container units for the Adelaide Festival. Surfside Hotel was his latest incarnation.

While we talked over all the major decisions together, I was happy to run with John's aesthetic judgement; he could 'see' better than me how an unimproved space would look when finished.

Orange, we decided, is the colour of Sri Lanka. From the Buddhist monks' robes to the legendary sunsets, from the umbrellas women carry as sun shields sashaying along the street in their saris, to the bunches of king coconuts sold from the backs of bicycles. Orange is everywhere. The colour blazes out, which is what we wanted to do on a crowded beachfront. For us, it represented joy, energy, and the colour of the tropics. So it became the hotel's signature colour.

Once decided, we went to Colombo on a mission – to find orange umbrellas in an outdoor furniture shop. We ordered six large rich-orange canvas sun umbrellas with teak frames for the beachside front of the hotel.

Now, with the umbrellas in place, it felt like showtime was in sight.

Chapter 9

TICK TOCK ON THE CLOCK

'Madame Dasha, excise police coming, coming right *now*. My friend messages me. He says they come to all bars in Hikkaduwa.'

Barman Vinod was shifting his lanky frame from foot to foot to foot. His large brown eyes widened with both the thrill of the drama and a genuine fear of the whispered warning he was giving me. Bar staff up and down the beach had been calling each other, warning the police were coming – Hikkaduwa's tom-tom phone drums were going into overdrive.

The local excise police randomly patrolled the beachfront bars, checking on the bar holder's permit to sell alcohol. Many little bars, like ours, didn't have and never would hold a licence to sell alcohol. And the excise police knew this. It was the monthly game of catch and collect.

Vinod's hissed message was the cue for us to vanish, to melt into the background pretending to be hotel guests. Vinod called up Nalinda to come and handle the police visit. John and I had entered Sri Lanka on tourist visas and were endlessly waiting for confirmation of our business visas as hospitality consultants.

Nick told us that the process was 'in train'. But until our business visas came through, we had no permit to work, so we could not be seen to be managing the hotel; even though all the staff and the neighbours knew we were doing just that.

We beat a retreat to our upstairs room, standing on our balcony sipping hastily poured glasses of Chilean wine, casually looking down over the courtyard. Observing what happens when Nalinda arrives to talk to the police posse.

Before we came to Sri Lanka, we knew we needed to navigate the potential liquor sales booby trap; we insisted on a clause in our agreement stating that Nalinda was the 'local liaison', responsible for all aspects of liquor supply and communication with the excise police. He ensured that the inspecting police received the monthly payment of around $US35 each, plus food and drinks.

No one blinked an eye.

This laissez-faire attitude towards paying the police and our lack of a proper visa was making me feel nervous, very nervous, as I silently concocted all the worst-case scenarios that ended up with us being banished and deported.

John savoured his drink unperturbed, accepting the bribery system as a given as he looked down into the courtyard.

'It's the way things are done.'

Cold comfort to my way of thinking.

At best, I saw this as tissue-thin protection for us because it primarily worked in the local owner's favour as an informal bribe system. But I suspected it could also be invoked, capriciously, against foreigners if required.

A new bar had appeared in the village some 300 metres along the beach and we had made friends with the charming owner, a clichédly handsome Frenchman, Jean, who'd arrived in Hikkaduwa around the same time we had. He'd run successful beach-hut bars in Goa, India, over the previous decade, and now he had his sights set on southwestern Sri Lanka as the 'new' hotspot for the international club set. He built a simple but sophisticated beach-hut bar – a circular cocktail bar surrounded by bar stools under a round thatched roof plonked right on the sand. With its uber-cool playlist, professional sound system and tiny dance floor cramming everyone together, Blue Moon bar soon became an instant hit; its Ibiza-style club vibe going off every night.

It was the go-to meat market for the lithe, gilded and skimpily dressed Euro-travellers. And making Jean and his business partner a lot of money. All in cash. The Sri Lankan-owned bars on either side of Blue Moon languished, with their former patrons flocking to Jean's cool new place.

Tuesday nights were the big marquee event, with sky-blue flyer handouts promising:

'DON'T STOP. MAKE IT POP...

... BUT THE PARTY DON'T STOP NO'

And if that wasn't enough to make the neighbouring bar owners seethe with jealousy over lost business and all-night noise, there was a coda on the flyer that was read as exclusionist by the locals. In much smaller letters: *Entrance free for foreigners.*

The word 'free' added fuel to an already simmering fire of locals feeling excluded from foreign-owned businesses. Although the $US5 entry fee would be regarded as low for tourists, it was beyond the pockets of most local Sri Lankans.

Some weeks after Blue Moon's opening, we propped up the bar, and asked Jean how business was going.

'Business is excellent, but the bar next door hates us. They're jealous and think we are stealing all their customers. So now the excise police keep demanding to see my visa and business documents. It's not good. The neighbours spread rumours about us that are lies. Saying we refuse to serve Sri Lankans. But I have all the right papers, so it should be okay.'

He shrugged with that Gallic cool and turned away to serve another customer.

Jean's experience set us asking each other whether or not jealousy could be described as a fundamental trait in Sri Lankan cultural behaviour, as it chimed with the experiences we'd had.

After trying out this theory on some local expats, we concluded that Sri Lankans knew this to be true, widely accepting jealousy and false accusations as part of a disposition they attributed to themselves – a cultural trait as defining as the British stiff upper lip, French superiority or Australian brashness.

Conversely, this idea seemed so outlandish because the Sri Lankans you meet are courteous, eager to please, respectful and charming.

The national Sinhalese flag carries the symbols of the four tenets Sri Lankans hold dear – kindness, friendliness, happiness, equanimity.

Were we imagining the power of jealousy based on a few sour grapes?

Googling 'Sri Lankans and Jealousy' I found a number of references to it as a cultural trait.

'I've found evidence of our theory about Sri Lankans and jealousy,' I told John, as he bit down on a piece of toast slathered in homemade marmalade.

'There's a university thesis written in the 1990s called "Conflict in Hierarchy: Jealousy Among the Sinhalese Buddhists". Lindy Warrell claims that the Buddhists of Sri Lanka describe themselves, collectively, as jealous people. In Sinhalese, she says it's called *okama irisiyawa, seroma irisiyawa*. Her informants described jealousy as the basis of Sinhalese culture.

She claims that workers, supervisors and managers commonly refer to it as the root of conflict in workplaces and villages.'

John was still crunching on his toast.

'Maybe jealousy kicks in when people see they're getting the raw end of the deal — that someone else is doing better than they are and has gotten a bigger slice of the pie. And that's when violence can erupt.'

John continued munching. 'Hmmm, I'm not convinced jealousy leads to violence. But, sure, it could make someone peddle false information to get revenge.

I reminded him, 'Remember how Nick warned us on our first visit to Sri Lanka – "Sri Lankans are usually a laid-back, peaceful lot. But they have a saying here, *when voices are raised, the machetes come out*".'

We weren't to know then how these words would return to haunt us.

I remembered, too, what one long-term Sri Lankan watcher said to me as we left Australia to come to Hikkaduwa – 'The tiger in the belly of the island can always become awakened by a trigger that comes out of nowhere.' I began to think that jealousy was perhaps another name for the tiger.

This intensity that ferments on islands fed into an ongoing discussion between us. How do islands shape and get a grip on people's imaginations?

They had undoubtedly captured ours, forging our sense of ourselves.

While we knew that islands could be places of enchantment, exoticism, mystery and beauty, we also knew they could be places of isolation and constraint. Islands had boundaries, defined by their coastlines and surrounded by the oceanic expanses of nothingness and busy trade routes that held us captive. Islands became places you had to fly away from, towards the promise of other worlds just over the horizon.

It was clear to us how Sri Lanka was defined by its geography and economics in the 21st century. It was blatantly an unequal economy that not everyone got to share. Despite its formative democratic socialist underpinnings as a republic, many missed out, leading to simmering jealousies, feuds and frustrations that created uneasy relationships that sometimes festered, leading to a backlash. The fight over its spoils forged Sri Lanka's history.

* * *

In his book *The Elephant Complex,* author John Gimlette writes:

> Everyone has wanted a piece of Paradise. The Tamils and the Sinhalese have contested this island for so long that no one can honestly say who got there first. To outsiders, the question may seem a dangerous irrelevance, but in Sri Lanka, it's been sparking off wars for over two thousand years. Indeed, looking back over the last two millennia, it is hard to spot a century in which Taprobane or Ceylon was neither occupied, invaded, nor riven by catastrophic civil war. Nor has it helped that there are always rich pickings for the predatory.

Gimlette goes on to quote the military historian Geoffrey Powell: 'Of course, a country doesn't have to be rich to invite invasions, but Ceylon was always wealthy: a treasure house of spices and gems, elephants and rice.'

Successive waves of colonial masters came to raid this treasure house – the Arabs, the Portuguese, the Dutch and the English – until, in 1978, it became the Democratic Socialist Republic of Sri Lanka. This trading history created a dynamic and multicultural mix of Muslims, Buddhist Sinhalese and Hindu Tamils, creating, in turn, a unique wealthy mixed-race class – the Burghers. Christian and English-speaking, they are the descendants of intermarriage between the Sinhalese and Portuguese and Dutch traders.

Broadly western educated, the Burghers include some of Sri Lanka's finest creatives. There are writers like expat Michael Ondaatje, who wrote the memoir *Running in The Family* and the Booker Prize-winning novel *The English Patient*, and award-winning expat novelist Michelle de Kretser who wrote *Questions of Travel*, *The Hamilton Case* and *The Life to Come*.

The visionary architect Geoffrey Bawa, called the father of 'Tropical Modernism', has influenced architecture throughout Asia and Australia, and comes from a Burgher background. His buildings are revelatory in their blending of the interior with the outside terrain while featuring the traditional architecture and building materials of Sri Lanka; buildings like the Heritance Kandalama Hotel nestle into the jungle, becoming part of it. Literally. Guests are warned about marauding monkeys and advised to close their windows at night.

The pioneering Barbara Sansoni and her son, Dominic, are also part of this coterie. They all represent talented and privileged Sri Lankans who had the resources to go away and extend their horizons beyond the island's boundaries. Those Burghers who returned to Sri Lanka were instrumental in forging a cultural elite.

But those mired in poverty (the World Bank estimates that nearly 40% of the Sri Lankan population lives below the poverty line), have been left suffering a lack of opportunities, magnified by the 26-year-long brutal civil war fought between the Sri Lankan government and the separatist Liberation Tigers of Tamil Eelam. Whole towns in the north of Sri Lanka were destroyed in the war, giving birth to one of the world's first female suicide bombers. A Black Tiger, seventeen-year-old Dhanu, killed herself and the former Prime Minister of India, Rajiv Gandhi, in Tamil Nadu on May 21, 1991.

After the country spent so long bearing witness to such vicious brutality, it felt to me that many people were drained of their humanity. Young men had resorted to joining the army during the conflict because they were too poor to have an alternative source of employment. But after the war finished, they were left shell-shocked, with no job skills, money or prospects. For many of these ex-army veterans, one of their only options was to work as security guards in a place like our hotel, where tourists would spend more on a night's accommodation than they could earn in a month.

Post-war, the Sri Lankan government launched a concerted push to sell the island internationally as 'peaceful', the latest paradise, the must-go-to tourist destination, and the site of 'escape, luxury and cultural tourism'.

Almost overnight, this push catapulted Sri Lanka from three war-torn decades of being economically crushed to unprecedented and accelerated prosperity. Paradoxically, the war safeguarded much of the island architecturally, preventing much of the rampant, unsustainable development seen throughout the rest of South-East Asia, in places like Bali and Thailand.

This made Sri Lanka an even more attractive marketing opportunity as an 'undiscovered' paradise.

From 2005, international investors swarmed and wooed the government of Mahinda Rajapaksa, with Chinese investors pouring millions upon millions into infrastructure. Australian billionaire, casino mogul James Packer, was granted an almost giveaway deal to build and create a casino hub in Colombo. Not that it ever eventuated.

Early on in our time in Sri Lanka, I gleaned a snippet of the Australian poet Robert Gray's 1993 poem 'Malthusian Island'. His insightful and prescient take on Sri Lanka:

> Paradise is always within walls; here it is in the hotel grounds or around some great bungalows, with their gardens and pools. Outside, there is wide purgatory ...

Seemed to echo just what we were trying to create.

* * *

We looked down at the empty courtyard, and with our wines drained, the way was clear for us to return. The excise police had moved on to the next place, leaving Vinod to sit mournfully behind the deserted bar. Nalinda, having sorted out the police, was nowhere to be seen.

Time to forget about the foibles of paradise and eat pizza down the road at the only Italian restaurant in the village. We needed to escape the hotel, our illegal status, and be tourists for an hour or so.

Chapter 10

THREE WEEKS TO GO

Two middle-aged men sat in their sarongs and perfectly ironed shirts, their legs folded sideways on the outside lounge floor area, painting two lots of kitchen shelving shiny white. Their brushes dipping in and out of the same large containers of white paint used to paint the corridor walls, the kitchen and the outside bar area. My nostrils flared on a sharp intake of breath as I saw tiny flecks of white paint dotting the polished concrete floor around them.

Better that John resolves this, I thought to myself.

I was learning that his instructions, man to man, were more likely to be acted on. And there was no point in my fretting about it. It's simply how it was.

Two more men were hard at work building a garden bed around the corner, one bordering it with small concrete blocks, the other digging up mounds of earth to plant the garden. A fridge mechanic was trying to revive our dying bar fridge, while an electrician was trying to coax the hotel's temperamental electrical wiring out of its episodic seizures. It was lunchtime, and impossible to find anywhere in the hotel that wasn't under construction with something being unbuilt or rebuilt.

The downstairs corridor walls had been painted white to make them look pristine, but the internet was still catastrophic. Despite the courteous and resourceful IT specialist, Nishan, who had been coming for four days to install WIFI boosters, the internet kept dropping out. For hours and hours at a time. Nishan threw his hands in the air, 'What to do? It's Sri Lankan Telecom's problem; they are sabotaging your service by slowing it down, they want you to upgrade to a newer, more expensive plan.' But Sri Lankan Telecom told us it's our equipment's fault. And round it went.

A carpenter was removing rudimentary old shelving from one of the eight downstairs budget accommodation rooms. Nalinda stood in the corridor watching, tight-lipped, his face locked in a peeved frown. He had built the shelving that was being removed and was complaining loudly, 'Why you take these shelves away? They good.'

He said he wanted all the wood to be used to build something else.

The old shelving ran along two walls taking up much-needed space in these small budget rooms. We had decided that it was better to use a wooden stand-alone clothes-and-towel rack that we could have made by a local furniture shop. The racks would complement our instant makeover – the newly painted mint-green walls, wooden clothes stands, hand-loomed green and white bedspreads made from cotton fabric I had sourced from Janasalu, the local women's weaving cooperative, new showerheads and toilet seats for the bathrooms and new aircon units installed. Instant refresh.

Nalinda carried some wooden shelving outside and loaded it into the hotel's tuk-tuk. He had told us that the vehicle was too old and delicate for any staff to drive. It required a special tuk-tuk licence, and, as we didn't speak Sinhala, neither John nor I were eligible to get one.

Standing in the corridor looking at the doors to the rooms, I clocked that there were no readable room numbers. I shot across the road to the woodcarver's shop and ordered small wooden squares carved with the individual numbers 1 to 15 to nail onto the doors.

The woodcarver sat cross-legged on the floor of his shop, polishing a carved, coiled-cobra wall piece, which he insisted on giving me for luck, to thank me for the numbers' commission. I was born in the Chinese zodiac year of the Snake, so took this as an omen of good fortune for our Sri Lankan venture.

Perhaps I was adopting local customs, as many Sri Lankans, including Nalinda, were superstitious, frequently consulting astrologers (usually Buddhist monks) to find the most auspicious times to conduct weddings, name children, build new houses, start new businesses, or undertake travel.

Whisperings from locals and expats say that the southwest of Sri Lanka, where our hotel is located, is well known for black magic, superstition, murder, mayhem and ruthless standover tactics.

Perhaps in the face of this, and as a result of a societal post-traumatic stress disorder after three decades of a brutalising civil war, people mostly adopted a 'don't know, don't rock the boat' attitude to any trouble or confrontation.

But equally, there could be sudden and inexplicable murderous outbursts. As Nick's mantra on our first visit to Sri Lanka described, 'Sri Lankans are very laid back, calm, peaceful people, but when voices are raised, the machetes come out.'

Rumours are currency in conversation in Sri Lanka, from our local tuk-tuk driver telling John with serious conviction, 'You know, Bob Marley's brother lives in Hikkaduwa,' to a story told to me by a café owner that took place near the village around the time we arrived.

A woman was found in a ditch, hacked to death with many machete blows. The police reported a death-by-suicide verdict. No one, not even her family, challenged it. 'But how is this possible to say suicide when her body was slashed with one, maybe more than one machete?' I ask Ari, the café owner.

'People too scared to be involved.'

The deceased woman lived across the busy Galle Road from our hotel on the so-called 'jungle side' of the village. Her neighbours said she was quarrelsome and difficult and although Sinhalese Buddhist, sometimes sported a red caste mark in sympathy with the Tamils. Alone, separated from her family and disliked by her community, she did own valuable land. Land that a powerful family had begun to build a luxury hotel on illegally. She took the family to court and was defeated. She dared to take them to a higher court and won.

Then her body was found cut to pieces.

Rumour said that her killers were out of the country within hours of the killing. Her son said he did not want the land or anything to do with it. People who knew her whispered this story to me. But none of them had seen the body. They only heard the rumours.

The next rumour I heard was that Grease Devils killed her. According to local legend, Grease Devils are thieves, wearing only underpants and covering their naked bodies in grease, making them impossible to grab hold of as they slide through the bars on windows. There had been newspaper and TV reports about a Grease Devil-panic that gripped central rural Sri Lanka when up to 30 incidents were reported of Grease Devils attacking young women at night, biting them on the necks and the breasts. Things escalated when police reported that two men, villagers identified as Grease Devils, were hacked to death by an angry mob in the central Sri Lankan village of Kotagala, in a tea-growing area.

The police tried to calm things down. 'There is no Grease Devil as such. It is a human among us with an ulterior motive of stealing or engaging in some illegal activities.' But people still believed Grease Devils were responsible for the attacks.

I came back from the woodcarver's shop to find John standing inside a roofless shed facing the sea at the side of the restaurant pavilion. Pulling a tape measure along the wall, measuring about three metres, he said, 'Sudith, this shelf here should be this long, big enough for surfboards.'

The carpenter looked at him blankly. John went out onto the beach to the Beach Break surf school gesturing to the peroxide-haired beach boy, idly gazing at the surf, and picked up a board, bringing it back into the shed.

'See this, Sudith? The shelf needs to hold a board like this one. And maybe longer boards. We need three shelves like this.' Sudith wobbled his head from side to side in the equivocal Sri Lankan way that, confusingly, neither confirms nor denies whether or not he agrees or understood.

Nick had told us that some of our guests, particularly the silver surfers from Australia, liked to bring their surfboards, so we figured we needed somewhere to stash them securely out of the way. Australian boards are highly prized, and surfers who bring their own treat them with the same consideration, love and care as their accompanying lovers and children. If not more so.

Before we took over the hotel, it looked like a low-budget dive with surfboards strewn over the floor, just inside the beachside doors. We converted this open-sided area into a TV lounge/library featuring a large glass-fronted bookcase, and made plans for the surfboard shed to be lock secured and the roof rebuilt to protect the boards from possible storms.

With the room numbers sorted and my head buzzing with the cacophony of building noise all around me, I figured it was the perfect time to go in search of a pair of carved stone welcome bowls. I was very taken by this nod to Buddhist tradition I'd seen in local boutique hotels. Matching stone bowls filled with water and floating flowers – frangipani and bougainvillaea blossoms – were placed at either side of the front door.

Nick had told us several times that Nalinda was a 'good Buddhist' and knowledgeable about Buddhist rituals, so I had consulted him about whether this simple gesture was appropriate for our hotel. Although surprised I should suggest it, he agreed that it would be. Even more so because we removed the old welcome sign from above the front door. Three letters had fallen off, leaving a message that seemed to contradict the intention: 'W lco.'

As I walked along the driveway past the hotel's front door, I saw an old painter wearing a perfectly pressed crisp white shirt over a sarong, bent over double, slowly walking backwards down the long corridor, carefully applying heavy-duty, shiny, grey pavement paint with a roller. I stopped to look, happy it was covering over the stained and scuffed ox-blood-coloured cement floor. The walls had already been painted bright white, and the light bulbs replaced in the floor's recessed squares lining the corridor. It's going to look pretty schmick, I thought, as I headed out the front to find our usual tuk-tuk driver propped outside.

We take off in the tuk-tuk, with Bob Marley blaring through the back doof-doof speakers on either side of my head:

'Get up. Stand up, stand up for your right

Get up. Stand up, don't give up the fight ...'

While this reggae call to arms reverberated through and around my head, a thought flashed into my mind like a lightning bolt: the painter hadn't barricaded the top entry to the corridor. Dogs, cats or people could be walking over the wet paint!

Already on the way towards Galle without a phone, I hoped somebody would see the problem.

I also hoped that by the time I got back, the electrician had fixed the wiring problem, so I wouldn't continue to get electric shocks every time I flicked on the light switches.

As the tuk-tuk streaked along the coast road, we sprinted past a roadside Buddha statue inside a glass display case with a flashing disco-style coloured halo behind its head. It reminded me that Buddhism's practice and interpretation are everywhere. From the ubiquitous three white prayer threads tied by the monks on people's right-hand wrists in return for a donation, through these disco Buddhas, to the large white stupas that could be seen at regular intervals along Galle Road.

* * *

In our hotel, the male staff would refer to young women as 'good' or 'bad'. Good girls were expected to display the Buddhist concepts of *lajja-baya* (respectability and modesty) and *sanwara* (good grooming, discipline, decency, control). In Sinhalese society, being of 'good' character is essential for a young woman to show that she is a good Buddhist and, therefore, marriageable. Reputation is everything, and fear of gossip rules.

I learned all about this when I decided I needed to learn Sinhala after hearing the language spoken around me and not comprehending a single word.

An economics student named Ashika arrived at the hotel one Saturday morning for our first lesson, chaperoned by her older brother. Around 21 years of age and very pretty in a reserved, demure way, she came armed with a children's alphabet book containing Sinhala's 58 letters. Her brother sat, a long way out of earshot, on one of the hotel sun lounges, but with her in his sightline.

Latith, our usually indifferent and lethargic waiter in his mid-twenties, rushed up, offering us tea. Something he had never done before. Ever. For me, or later for our hotel guests. John or I would usually have to prise him off his stool in front of the bar with, 'Go and ask them what they'd like to order.'

Seeing his unusually enthusiastic reaction, I teased him that he might be interested in Ashika as girlfriend material. 'No no no, Madame Dasha. I have a girlfriend, and anyway, Ashika is a "good" girl.'

Latith thought it normal and desirable that unmarried Ashika would be out and about under the watchful protection of her brother. However, it didn't stop them from flirting and making eyes at each other over the coming weeks. As Ashika valiantly endeavoured to teach me Sinhala, it reinforced that this expectation of restraint and respectability was not applied to young men.

While I discovered these principles through my lessons in the Sinhala language, it didn't advance my linguistic proficiency. At all. The beauty of the circular hieroglyphic characters in the Sinhalese Brahmic script captivated me, but reproducing and understanding the language eluded me beyond a few basic phrases. My ear couldn't equate it with any other language I'd ever heard. The characters swirled in front of me, like the eyes of the cartoon characters Ren and Stimpy.

* * *

The intense pleasure of feeling the warm, scented, humid air on my face as Chinthaka's tuk-tuk sped past yet another disco Buddha in a raised glass box spurred more musings about the worldly interpretation of local Buddhist practice. When I asked Vinod one day if he was going to the Buddhist temple to pray on the full moon (Poya Day), he answered, 'Oh yes, Madame

Dasha. I go to pray for more money, more service charge and more money.'

Other elements of Sri Lankan Buddhist practice confounded us too, John in particular. He struggled with the notion that the Sinhala state co-opted Buddhism to underpin its war cry. He was shocked to find that from the early 1990s, Buddhist monks entered provincial councils and then parliament on a platform that was akin to ethnic cleansing.

Over 75% of the population was Sinhalese Buddhist, while the remaining people were Hindu Tamils, Muslims or Christians. John tried to get his head around the notion that monks, some of them blatantly racist and anti-Tamil, meddled in temporal politics. It seemed impossible to reconcile that Buddhism's pacifist image could be associated with sectarian aggression. It was shocking to discover that the Buddhist monks elected to parliament pressed for, amongst others, the Sri Lankan army to wipe out the Tamil Tigers as a 'final solution to the civil war.'

In his 2015 book, *This Divided Island*, Samanth Subramanian wrote that some monks even took off their robes and took up arms to fight the Tigers. John reminded me that, memorably, a Buddhist monk shot Prime Minister Bandaranaike in 1959. 'For the country, race and religion,' he shouted as he was dragged away, leaving the dying Prime Minister urging people not to harm the monk in any way.

Like many westerners, John and I had always believed Buddhism to be a religion of peace and found these contradictions mind-numbingly challenging to reconcile. Wasn't one of the Five Moral Precepts of Buddhism abstaining from harming living beings? Not according to Samanth Subramanian:

> The Sinhalese like to think of their Buddhism as muscular ... Sinhalese Buddhism is a coiled and wary creature, its reflex always to be aggressive in defence. Since 2006 when the Sri Lankan government had started winning the war, and after its victory in 2009, this ready Buddhist aggression had fused with military triumphalism.

This came home to both of us in a 2013 YouTube clip showing 30 Buddhist monks leading around two hundred men on a rampage against a local Christian church in Hikkaduwa. Monks were urging the men to break down the high metal fence and force their way in, while a small group of policemen looked on, powerless to act. No one was arrested, despite extensive damage and threats to the priests' lives. Later a police spokesman claimed, 'A mistake was made in failing to deploy adequate officers to guard the churches.'

It appeared that we lived in a country guarded by saffron-robed warriors defending their faith.

When John and I talked about this dichotomy between practice and belief in Sri Lankan Buddhism, I began to feel queasy that the potential for violence could seemingly erupt out of the teachings of peace and well-being. I wondered whether we really knew what lay beneath the calm surface of our staff's smiles and deference.

In contrast, Nalinda's discomfort and displeasure at our changes were only too apparent. Nick's remark reverberated around us again, 'When voices are raised, machetes come out.'

When I arrived at the stoneware stall on the road to Galle, I found two matching black cast-cement welcome bowls, loaded them onto the floor of the tuk-tuk and turned back to return to the relentless daily schedule. The paradoxes of Sri Lankan Buddhism were relegated to swirling in the background as the staccato demands of the hotel's refurbishment competed for our attention.

When I got back, the mechanic declared the bar fridge terminally dead. The concrete pavers in the courtyard had been laid down to form an outdoor, grid-like terrace with buffalo grass laid between the squares, and the new aircon units had been installed in all the rooms, replacing the old ceiling fans.

As we hurtled around the spinning wall of death towards showtime, it was actually beginning to feel like we'd make it.

Chapter 11

BLOW THE HOUSE DOWN

Sophie was already in the sky, flying to Sri Lanka from Barcelona, when the sky opened up, dumping solid sheets of monsoonal rain all afternoon. Hail fell so hard it bounced back, knee high, off the courtyard stones.

After dark, a raging typhoon ripped through the hotel. Rolling thunder cracked, crashed and rumbled at eardrum-splitting levels right above us. Jagged, multi-forked lightning stabbed the sea and strafed the sky. A terrifying light show with the scariest soundtrack I ever did hear. The kind of show that would feature Iron Maiden's vocalist, Bruce Dickinson, underscoring the end of the world, screaming at ear-splitting decibels 'For the Greater Good of God' over the band's driving, apocalyptic, heavy metal beats. Terrifying. We had never been in the eye of a storm like this.

Howling winds surrounded us, whirling like deranged dervishes. John and I lay rigid on our bed, side-by-side, clasping each other's hands with a vice-like grip, each of us able to feel the other's blood beating in fear. One more cracking explosion shuddered through the building. Way, way too close. I shot off the bed, diving into the bedroom next door, sliding sideways under the wooden bed frame and yelled at John to follow me. He scrambled after me, perching on the bed I was lying under.

'John, John, what's happening? Are we safe? Are the balcony doors going to blow out?'

'Dunno. Hope not.'

He looked down the corridor towards our seafront bedroom, the blackened sea was strobe lit by lightning as the rain lashed sideways, pouring a torrent of water into the room through the gap between the bottom of the glass door and the floor. Springing into action, John grabbed all the towels he could find, frantically trying to stop the deluge. It didn't work. Water poured in, creating an instant – and rising – indoor pool.

John waded out of the room, going to see what had happened. I emerged, crablike, from under the bed and sat on it, dazed. He came back 15 minutes later, his face drained of colour with his eyes bulging behind his yellow glasses.

'We've taken a hit. There's a big hole downstairs in the corridor roof; the ceiling has been smashed through and there's a huge lump of concrete on the hallway floor.'

This was the corridor we had just carefully painted two days before. Ruined.

Exhausted and dismally damp, we fell into a bed in an empty room. Nothing could be done immediately, and we told ourselves it was better to wait until daylight to do anything.

Early morning, we awoke to a startling sight. A massive sheet of asbestos was hanging off the tall courtyard palm, dangling like a Damoclean sword, just waiting to drop on someone. And judging by the other largish bits of smashed asbestos roofing on the ground, we'd also taken a big hit on the front upstairs balcony roof. Our premium rooms on offer were ruined.

John looked around at the disaster-strewn courtyard and turned to me, saying, 'Well, I guess those guys will know whether their insurance pays for acts of God or Buddha!'

He emailed the news to Nick in London. Short and to the point:

> *Between the electrical wiring catching fire, shocks from faulty plugs and switches and flying rocks and asbestos sheeting, we ain't feeling very comfortable!!!! And the forecasts seem to be for even worse storms tomorrow night. More when we know more.*

Chapter 12

TOO MANY COOKS

The typhoon was still howling the following day as sheets of fat rain pelted down. The sky hung low over Colombo airport like a wet, grey carpet. Sophie struggled into the arrivals hall, her lean, compact frame walking lopsided, weighed down under two enormous striped plastic bags. Seeing me running towards her, she dropped the bags and flicked her shoulder-length dark hair from across her face. We hugged each other tightly.

'I can't believe you've made it! Look at you!'

Sophie pulled away. 'Dasha! This stuff of yours weighs a tonne.'

She pushed one of the bags towards me. 'This one's got John's dream machine – the ice-cream maker. I got it on Amazon. So now it's flown from the UK to Spain to Sri Lanka. Hopefully, it's still in one piece! And all I've brought is a bikini, a sarong, what I've got on and some chef whites. That's it. All the rest of this stuff is equipment for you.'

As we hurtled south towards Galle, down the country's first and only smooth new tollway, Sophie was introduced to Sri Lanka's landscape. Blurry, wet glimpses of rubber plantations, cinnamon forests, the occasional mysterious Buddhist stupa peaking over the tops of the forests and green, green, green paddy fields all whizzed by. She was yet to find out what a luxury this was – not to drive on the backbreaking, potholed, rutted roads all over the rest of the island.

Trying to set our hotel scene for her, I launched into an introduction. 'Don't laugh when you hear the staff calling us Mr John and Madame Dasha. It wasn't our idea. They all did it. We tried to push the "we're all working together line, so please call us John and Dasha". But in the next sentence, it was Mr John and Madame Dasha. Again. Again and again. No matter what we said. After a few days, we gave up. Too hard. And maybe they want that formality. It's ingrained here, that line between the boss and the staff, by foreigners and Sri Lankans alike.'

The rain was pounding the roof of our hotel's eight-seater van, while Sujith, the driver, kept turning up the Sri Lankan pop radio station to try and drown it out.

I raised my voice against the background noise, 'You know, in tourist towns like Hikkaduwa, foreigners are seen as potential wallets. No matter how equal we might want to be. Or think we are. There are two prices for everything, depending on where you're from. That's just the way it is.'

Sophie listened, nodding.

With the windscreen wipers slapping time, she was suddenly distracted, pointing through the window, 'Dasha, that's just ridiculous!'

A man was riding his motorbike alongside us, utterly drenched. One hand clutched an open umbrella over his head; the other was on his bike's throttle while the rain came at him sideways.

I tell her about the new staff we've hired, explaining that chef Adith is looking forward to working on a menu that's not just the traditional curry and rice. 'Well,' says Sophie, 'the only way I can understand the food is to go into the kitchen, cook alongside them and go to the market with them. I want to sit with them, pound the spices and learn their recipes. Working with Adith is like going on a gastronomic holiday for me.'

Ours was a collaboration born out of deep friendship and culinary adventure that would be tested to the max before it was over. And Nick had no money to pay her.

We pulled off the main road into our hotel's gravel driveway to find the building buzzing with action. The monsoonal downpour had tailed off into a drizzle curtain with John standing under the roof of the courtyard verandah, wrangling the traffic of the hotel painters, the carpenters, the furniture repairers and the gardeners all criss-crossing over each other. As Sophie stepped from the entrance hallway into the courtyard, he enveloped her petite frame with his tall bulk in a bear hug.

'It's so great to see you, big man. I brought the ice-cream maker. Jaggery ice cream coming up.'

John's latest obsession was to make jaggery ice cream for our restaurant after he had devoured it in the up-market Colombo hip spot, Paradise Road. Jaggery is a specialty of Sri Lanka, a honey-coloured palm sugar made from the crystallised sap of the kithul flower from the fishtail palm tree. Its delicate caramel flavour can be turned into a syrup traditionally poured over a sensational buffalo milk yoghurt that the Sri Lankans call curd. Flavouring ice cream with jaggery took the notion of caramel to a whole new mouth-blowing level.

'How is it here?' Sophie asked, looking around the platoon of workers sitting on their haunches, painting shelving, hammering and cutting up wood while the rain continued pouring down. Two guys on the roof were trying to put new asbestos sheets in place, while other hotel staff milled around in the rain-battered courtyard.

'You'll see, it's like trying to wrangle smoke,' he answered, pulling out of their embrace. I caught John's glance over Sophie's shoulder. He shook his head almost imperceptibly.

I knew what that meant. There was a cash flow crisis, with Nick's promised investors' money still not materialising. With no ready cash, buying kitchen equipment, or anything else, was on hold until the funds appeared.

'Where's the kitchen?' asked Sophie, brimming with expectation.

The three of us entered the long shipping-container-shaped kitchen space, with its scuffed white tiled bench along one wall and windows above it.

Sophie reached out to touch the long, narrow metal-framed stove. It wobbled like jelly, teetering at her touch. Five gas burners sat on top of a metal frame connected to two gas bottles on the floor.

'John,' she barked, 'this is an accident waiting to happen. The first thing we do is fix this cooker because someone will knock it over, and it'll burn the place down.' She swivelled. Taking it all in, 'I've never seen a kitchen in worse condition. It's not even a kitchen. It's a room with something dangerous in the middle of it. Where's the running water?

'Ahhhh ... it's outside the kitchen door. It's not hot. But,' he continued as he ushered her outside, 'we're planning to run hot water into the sink out here, so the plates can at least be washed.'

A trail of eight hotel staff had followed each other into the kitchen to make themselves a cup of tea.

'What are they all doing in here?' Sophie demanded, looking at John.

'Morning tea time,' answered chef Adith.

'Well, that's got to stop. Right now. We're moving the urn out of the kitchen to the bar. Now.'

Turning to Adith, Sophie snapped into her best Gordon Ramsey impersonation, 'We only have the cooking staff in the kitchen. No one else.'

John introduced her, 'Adith, this is the new boss chef, Sophie.'

She offered her hand to Adith. 'That's very flattering, but it's not the case. We're collaborating here, and I'm not going to step on your toes. You're chef number one, and I'm here to help.'

Adith nodded, clearly understanding that she was the boss, his wide-open smiling face indicating his easy-going acceptance. He introduced her to his tall, gawky son-in-law, Ari, as his sidekick – second chef. We later came to see that Ari's lack of kitchen rhythm turned him into the hapless, accident-prone half of a comedy duo, always in the wrong place at the wrong time.

Early next morning, Sophie – her hair scraped back into a ponytail and dressed in her chef's whites – marched purposefully across the courtyard into the kitchen with a determined look. She was ready for business.

The standard local meal was a Sri Lankan fish, chicken or vegetable curry served with red rice, lentil dahl, chutney, and a pappadam; one that western tourists tired of eating every day. Sophie and Adith agreed that they would experiment with the menu by mixing classic Mediterranean elements like rich Italian tomato salsa poured over eggplant with a char-grilled chicken breast, alongside the famous Sri Lankan whole crab in coconut curry sauce served with yellow rice. Their aim was for a modern fusion menu of Sri Lankan and Mediterranean cuisine.

Sophie and Adith went daily to the local, open-air fruit and vegetable market where she was introduced to some unfamiliar vegetables.

'This one, Sophie, is like your spinach. We use it to make mallum, a kind of warm salad. We cook it with freshly grated coconut, turmeric, some lime juice, onion and a small green chilli.'

This made it to our menu, as Sri Lankan-style grilled chicken and warm spinach salad. Adith also introduced Sophie to the delicious locally-produced buffalo paneer (cottage cheese). They devised a dish together: fresh prawns in spicy tomato sauce with homemade buffalo paneer.

We knew that a successful restaurant would draw people away from the beach, make money and raise the hotel's profile. We had to get it right. Adith had found us a reliable fish supplier so fresh seafood became our big-ticket menu item.

Sophie fast discovered that what she was asking of Adith and Ari, and what she thought they all agreed to, was not necessarily what was being done, particularly around food handling:

'Chef, Ari, the clams have to be fresh. We buy them fresh in the morning and serve them fresh for lunch and dinner. We cannot put them in the freezer. Ever. Okay?' They had both nodded vigorously. Sophie thought they were in agreement.

But she was being introduced to the complexity of the Sri Lankan nod, where the head moves from side to side. As Westerners we assume that Sri Lankans are nodding in agreement. But it's more ambiguous than that. The speed of the nod can be an indicator, as can the position of the brows. It can mean, 'I've heard what you have said to me, but I'm unconvinced.' Or simply, 'I'm registering that I've heard what you have to say.'

It rarely indicates agreement. Perhaps Sophie had a sixth sense about this, because having told them both about the clams, she drew Adith aside.

'Chef, can you make sure Ari understands what I'm saying? It's important. We can't put fresh clams in the freezer overnight and cook them the next day. They'll be like rubber. Clams in garlic and lemon needs to be one of our signature dishes, and it's gotta be fresh.'

'Yes, yes, yes,' nodded Chef Adith, vigorously waggling his head from side to side. The following day Sophie opened up the freezer.

'Chef, what are these clams doing in the freezer? We never put the clams in the freezer. We buy them fresh every day, and if we still have some left by the end of the day, we throw them out. Or you take them home. If they're not fresh, we don't serve them. Okay?'

'Yes, yes,' he nods.

The next day and the day after that, and then the day following that, the leftover clams went back in the freezer to be served up as little rubber bullets.

By the fifth day, we dropped fresh clams in lemon and garlic, Italian style, from the menu. Too hard. Wasteful notions of western gourmet taste were no match for Sri Lankan frugality. Or the Sri Lankan nod.

We replaced the clams with Sophie's whitebait recipe from her book *My Barcelona Kitchen*. It worked a treat, presenting tiny crispy fried fish on Sri Lankan betel nut leaves, served with a Catalan romesco sauce made from roasted capsicums, almonds, cayenne pepper and olive oil.

'Now that's fusion cooking,' we proudly told ourselves.

But there were some mysteries we never got to the bottom of. Literally. The old kitchen freezer was one.

With Sophie watching, John lifted the detached lid on the battered, rust-flecked freezer. 'Chef, we need this all cleaned out by tomorrow. Nobody knows how long this food's been in here.'

'Yes, yes. All cleaned by tomorrow.' Chef Adith nods. Sophie: 'Are you promising me?'

'Yes, Yes,' nodded Adith.

He and Sophie took out the ancient frozen items, put them into a cardboard box, and then put the box out next to the rubbish.

Next day. Sophie opened the freezer to put in her freshly made ice cream, but the same old pieces of discarded frozen food are all back in the freezer.

'Chef, what's this? Did we not take this out last night?'
Adith: 'Yes, Chef.'
'To throw out?'
'Yes, Chef, but...'
'No but *nada* ... take it home and give it to your family but get rid of it.'
'But it's frozen, Chef ... it's good.'
'So can we use it for staff food?'
'But Chef, not sure ... not safe ... but it's good...'
'So we throw it out?'
'Yes, Chef.'
'When?'
'Tomorrow ...'

The next day, and the days after, it was still there – not safe, but good, frozen.

Because of the frequent power cuts, it was impossible to know how often the stuff in the freezer had been frozen, unfrozen, and frozen again. Let alone how many weeks, months or longer it had been in the freezer.

Despite the rubber bullet clams and the freezer wars, Sophie and Chef Adith developed an easy, respectful rapport working together. They would stand side by side in the kitchen, slicing, cutting, and pounding as they discussed the menu.

'Adith, the kitchen is limited, so we can't put many different dishes on the menu. We'll offer choices for a four-day stay so that everyone can eat something different for an entrée and a main. We'll always have a curry of the day, and there have to be the same standards for every dish, so people come to expect fresh, simple, beautifully-prepared food.'

Adith nodded vigorously.

'The big specials on our menu will be your wonderful chilli crab and those spectacular jumbo prawns, because they are just so fresh.'

Every morning, a young man peddled up the side of the hotel on his bicycle with the catch of the day glistening in his front cane basket. He mostly wore a pink T-shirt featuring a large fish with a cock-eye, which was disconcerting as he has a turned eye, making it seem like he is always looking over his shoulder. Or, when he showed off two giant tunas, dangling by their tails, one in each hand, he's looking at both of them. Every day this ritual was repeated, with mouth-watering freshness, straight from the nearby fish markets at Dodanduwa.

It wasn't just the hotel guests the kitchen was cooking for. Eight hotel staff needed to be fed – every day. Grandmotherly Mrs Prema used all her ingenuity as a cook to provide for them because of the limited resources available to her. Her talent lay in creating delicious meals for the staff out of just the scraps the chef allowed her to have.

The young men referred to her as Mother. Squat, broad-faced with a buck-toothy smile and a long grey plait. Chef Adith was very strict about what she could use, 'Sophie, only leftovers for staff meals. Mrs Prema cannot use food bought for guests' meals. She can make them tuna fish curry with the kingfish bones and vegetable peelings.' Coconut shavings would be toasted to form the basis of a curry.

Per Sri Lankan domestic custom, Mrs Prema always removed her shoes before entering the kitchen, leaving them outside. Not used to ever seeing bare feet in a restaurant kitchen, Sophie decided this wasn't on. Everyone had to wear shoes. For health and safety reasons, she explained. The kitchen staff all nodded in agreement, but Mrs Prema continued to leave her shoes outside the kitchen door, and Sophie kept telling her to go and put them on. We even bought her new shoes to be her 'kitchen shoes'. But no go.

Over the next two days, the more Mrs Prema didn't wear her shoes in the kitchen, the more Sophie insisted. A losing battle. Finally, Chef said to her quietly, 'Sophie, big trouble coming!'

It was Chef's way of alerting Sophie to potential problems, meaning, 'Heads up, this could be an issue, and you need to resolve it before it blows up.'

Or, 'Back off; you're not going to win this one.'

Like Sophie, I was concerned about the fate of Mrs Prema's bare feet, but John laughed uproariously when I told him this story at breakfast a few days later.

John always saw the funny side in most things in our lives, and I always saw potential potholes. We both decided it's 'Big Trouble Coming' every day, and it became our running gag.

It wasn't just the lack of shoes that had Sophie on alert. One morning we were sipping our tea together in the courtyard when she looked askance.

'Dasha, he's got to stop fondling his balls all the time,' indicating with her head backwards at one of the housekeepers. He was absent-mindedly stroking his genitals through his sarong while gazing out to sea, standing outside the kitchen facing the restaurant. We resolved that it would be best if John had a quiet word with him.

* * *

A month after we arrived in Sri Lanka, Nalinda, his family, two dogs, and a cat, moved out of the hotel. Progress had slowed on the house that Nalinda was building for his family and he had kept putting off moving into the temporary accommodation Nick arranged for them.

It was an extremely awkward time together under one roof, as we worked at breakneck speed to get the hotel ready to re-open. We knew it could be tricky having Nalinda there, but we had to put up with it once we arrived.

We were more than acutely aware of Nalinda's sense of displacement with us managing the hotel. To sweeten the deal further, Nick had given him a small ownership percentage stake, which made Nalinda Nick's business partner in the hotel.

Perhaps we should have been more alert to what these changes meant to Nalinda. The clues were there. When John was designing and printing business cards, he asked Nalinda if he wanted to have a personalised card, and Nalinda said yes. He wanted the words managing director above his full name printed on his card. This only added to the confusion about whether he was working with us as local liaison, as we thought, or whether he genuinely believed that we were working for him.

During this first month, when we were dealing with the unbearable stress of monies not being made available, the bar being rebuilt from scratch and the kitchen still inoperable with no running water, communication with Nalinda grew more clogged, haphazard and unreliable.

Nalinda was an enthusiastic amateur chef and had sometimes cooked for the hotel. He had designed the large multi-burner metal structure that Sophie deemed a death trap, and watched with great alarm as it was dismantled into half its size. He constantly complained to the staff about the new menu, 'Not enough curries.' He was also very suspicious about the chef's fish supplier, going so far as to loudly accuse the chef of getting a kickback for using him.

Meanwhile, all action had come to a halt when things went wrong – and we relied on Nalinda's help to fix this stuff, but he didn't.

The internet service was atrocious. Sometimes it dropped out for hours, day after day, causing the vast frustration that only digital impotence can.

In many instances, it wasn't only the internet that went down; it was the power supply in the hotel. Everything went off. Blackout. When called to help, Nalinda explained that it wasn't a hotel problem but a supply problem to the area. While sometimes true enough, it didn't explain why the hotel on either side of us had power when we often didn't. There was also still the same problem with the light switches in the restaurant – they gave off electric shocks when you flicked them on.

Most mornings, John and I breakfasted together around seven. We discussed where we were up to and what needed to be done, both of us surprised at how symbiotically we worked together.

Thinking about the mounting obstacles one morning, I hazarded a guess, 'Do you think Nalinda doesn't want to help us? Do you think he feels we've pushed him out?'

'Hmmm ... I don't think it's that so much, more like him doing everything at the last minute and not being used to communicating what he's doing to other people. I don't think it's wilful. Or I hope it isn't.' John had more faith than me.

We would see how that turned out.

The hotel was a glorious location for breakfast, with the restaurant tables facing open-sided onto the courtyard and the beachfront. Like most local hotels, we offered a choice of a Sri Lankan breakfast – two curries, a fish and dahl, with fresh coconut sambal and a couple of rotis – or, guests could have the 'Euro version' of toast, fresh fruit and curd (yoghurt) with jaggery syrup. John always stuck to the latter while I grew increasingly passionate about the former because of the fresh coconut sambal, made by pounding together freshly grated coconut, tomatoes, garlic, lime juice, coriander and chilli. I became convinced that the sambal must be an aphrodisiac, as it had the most intoxicating moreish effect. You just can't get enough. John remained unconvinced, slyly asking, 'What are you telling me?

Chapter 13

THE TEMPERATURE'S RISING

The unrelenting march to opening day became more frenzied, with tempers getting shorter. And shorter. And shorter.

One morning, I went to Galle, hunting for 10 colour-matched new toilet seats. But after combing the building supply shops, finding just one matching set, let alone 10 of any colour, proved impossible. When I arrived back with six seats in different shades of cream, Sophie was sitting on the couch outside the kitchen. Arms crossed emphatically across her chest; her face was scrunched in a frown, giving off sulphurous fumes of fire and fury.

'Everything okay?' I squeaked, as it most obviously wasn't.

'No, it's not. I can't do this.' she blurted out.

'What seems to be the problem?' I asked, in my best telephone counsellor voice.

'I need money. There's no food for the staff. The chef's got 10 hungry mouths looking at him. When I asked John about it, he just walked off, saying, "No". Because the money you guys are waiting on still hasn't come through. This is just impossible.'

She erupted. 'John has to understand I'm a consultant here. Not an employee. I'm here to consult. That's the reason I'm here. If you don't want to hear my information, fine. I'll go and lie on the beach. But I'm not going to spend all this energy and be treated like this. It's not on.'

'I understand. Let me have a quiet word with him. Please understand how much we value you being here, particularly since you're not being paid. Your being here is a great gift to us.'

I completely understood. Sophie was really doing us a favour and we needed her desperately. Alarmed, I went to find John to broker a solution to these high-noon kitchen dramatics. I found him standing in the alleyway, on the other side of the kitchen from where Sophie was sitting and fuming. He was on the phone.

'Nalinda, the gully trap outside the kitchen is blocked. Again! I'm worried the sewage sludge coming out of it will flood the kitchen. Big health risk for everybody. Chef says that if the sewerage floods into the kitchen, that's it. He can't cook.'

From the kitchen doorway that opened onto the side alley, I was horrified by the rising ankle-deep disaster. I could only hear John's side of the conversation, which sounded strained and emphatic. And he was losing patience. 'I know the drain fixer came two days ago, but it's not working.'

His voice rose. 'Can you get them to come back again? Today?'

But by the look on his face as he listened to Nalinda's answer, it wasn't going to happen. Hmm ... Not the best moment to try and coax an apology out of him.

Like everything else in the hotel, the old sewerage pipes struggled to keep up. And it wasn't just the kitchen leaking. Two nights before, it had rained. Torrentially. The hotel roof leaked all over the bed in the top floor top-dollar sea-view balcony room. Roof leaks sprung up over the manager's rooms we were finishing off, so we could move into them. Now, with water plopping into buckets and spreading across the floor, so much for moving in. Worse, the rain poured over the new electrical wiring, sending more bad shocks through the switches when we flicked them on. Again.

It felt like the leaky ship we were sailing in was sinking before it had even been launched.

For John, the most challenging part of navigating this ship was Nalinda's reluctance to address any of these problems. When told the hot water had gone off without warning, he claimed that 'the hot water stops when it rains ...' Not that we understood why, as there was no further explanation.

When John called about the roof leaks, Nalinda said, 'Call Nick, tell him the problem.' Which makes no sense as Nick lives in London. The sometimes great notion of working together as a team with Nalinda was quickly evaporating.

Later that afternoon, I cajoled John into making an apology to Sophie to calm things down. The very next day Nalinda announced that the missing investor's money had finally come through into the hotel's bank account.

We had cash flow.

Big Trouble not coming immediately.

It was perfect timing as we only had a few days left with Sophie before she was due to fly back to Barcelona. It had always been a tough ask of her to get the kitchen and the menu up and running in the space of 10 days. But we did it and held on to our friendship which was strengthened because of it. When she left we had an unbreakable bond because of what we had achieved together.

* * *

It's fair to say that in our fever to follow our dream of one last grand adventure together, John and I hadn't really investigated the consequences of coming to Sri Lanka. We'd never been adept at risk assessment, but we were always up for seizing opportunities. Perhaps it was a mix of that Aussie 'She'll be right mate' approach, stirred with equal parts 'Ignorance is bliss,' and a twist of 'Ahhhh, let's just go for it!'

While some solutions to the hotel's problems were obvious, other issues bubbled away unseen beneath the surface, bursting and catching us off guard later on, no matter how sure we were that we were ready for any and everything.

The countdown hit kick-off, and the big day was on us.

Chapter 14

AT LAST

7 am.

Jayantha and Oshan opened up the four large teak-framed umbrellas in their 'look at me' brilliant orange along the beachfront.

7.30 am.

'Latith, we can't have ashtrays on the table. Our guests don't want to smoke at breakfast and they won't want to sit next to anyone smoking. Please take them back to the bar.'

I had had this conversation several times already, but needed to tell him again. Today of all days. Latith sloped back to the bar, juggling a pile of ashtrays while looking at the ground.

8 am.

I did a last survey of the restaurant's tables, set and dressed in their new orange linen tablecloths, as half a dozen guests ambled into the open-sided pavilion for our first breakfast service. Suresh, the housekeeper, plugged in the USB stick that's supposed to have the chilled-out Ibiza style playlist, *Breakfast*.

Instead of languid ocean-wash beats, a high-volume frenetic salsa boomed out of the sound system, pulsing a heart-stopping beat with a screeching trumpet of Arturo Sandoval. The guests in the restaurant looked like bug-eyed cartoon characters, hair standing on end with startled nerves shattered.

I hurtled over to the sound system, turning it down with a savage fade and inspected the ribbon attached to the USB stick. It read *Cocktail*. Designed to get everybody in the happy hour party mood, drinking cocktails and feeling the fun. 'Suresh, wrong stick, wrong stick.' My words tumble out, 'We need the *Breakfast* stick. The one I showed you.'

He shrugged and averted his panther-like eyes towards the beach. 'Sorry, Madame Dasha, I put *Breakfast* in tomorrow.'

Over the previous two weeks, I had lovingly made playlists for the different times of day, drawing from a list of 2000 songs a DJ friend gave us. Each playlist was put onto a separate USB stick with a colour-coded ribbon with the mood word written in black. A green ribbon with *Reggae*, a red ribbon that says *Cocktail*, a blue ribbon for *Breakfast* sounds and yellow for *Dinner*. I explained to Suresh what each stick was and when it should be played, I thought successfully because he nodded his head from side to side.

I look up to see Chef summoning me wildly through the glass window, pointing theatrically into the outside passageway that ran alongside the kitchen.

'Rat,' he whispered conspiratorially.

Playing host to rats simultaneously as paying guests would be the death knell of our nascent hotel business.

On Chef's advice, we invested high hopes in a Buddhist rat trap bought from the local supermarket. A small cage-like contraption, it was supposed to lure the rat in, then allow it to be transported, as a sentient being, to another destination of the Buddhist trapper's choice. Not killed. Out of sight, out of mind.

This worked only as long as the rats played along. And, being intelligent creatures, there were no guarantees.

Happily, one did get caught later that morning. It was carried across the maniacal traffic in front of the hotel to the other side of the road and released down a side street. No way a rat could survive that murderous traffic if it planned on returning.

With the ever-present tiny black-striped squirrels and the occasional mongoose running the gauntlet along the top of the hotel's fence line, we hoped we could rely on them as a distraction, or optical illusion, to allay any guests' concerns should any other rats show up.

The indigenous palm squirrels (*Lena* in Sinhala) have long bushy tails and adorable small velvet fold-back ears. They are the same size and shape as the resident rats (except for their plush tails), belonging to the same class of mammals, Order Rodentia. But the squirrels engendered a very different response in guests. They are seen as cute, exotic, endearing, and not 'rodent-like' in the least. Sri Lankan novelist Michelle de Kretser wrote about them beautifully in *The Hamilton Case*:

> Her stillness attracted birds, chameleons, the little squirrels whose striped backs showed where they had been stroked by a god's fingers.

We resolved to stick with that description.

The breakfast service rolled out with Latith serving four guests the classic Sri Lankan breakfast. The only problem was that the guests thought they were getting toast, boiled eggs, butter and jam. Poking suspiciously at the food with a spoon, a neat, sandy-haired Englishman in a lemon polo shirt asked, 'What is this?' in an injured tone.

John swept in, employing his best charm force-field, trying to sell the idea that the guest and his equally neat wife could begin their holiday with an authentic Sri Lankan culinary experience. But they weren't buying. John took the breakfasts back to the kitchen to reset the order and to check on the progress of the Buddhist rat cage.

Sitting down together after the guests had finally been served and finished their breakfasts of choice, John and I looked at each other, unsure what to say without bursting out laughing.

'Well, we're open. We've gotten this far. Now there's just lunch and then dinner to get through...' I felt a little limp, hunched over a cold cup of tea, replaying the comedy of breakfast errors in my mind.

Tomorrow can only get better.

Lunch is where we needed to lure passing people from the beach, as our hotel guests were generally out and about, so we were thrilled when an urbane, sophisticated Spanish couple, Roberto and Jorge, popped up off the beach at lunchtime. Settling themselves into a surfside table, they looked around. 'We like your sign on the beach. Looks good.' It's working!

Our sharp new sandwich board signs stuck in the sand out front promised:

RESTAURANT NOW OPEN
MODERN SRI LANKAN CUISINE & DRINKS
IN OUR BEACHSIDE GARDEN

John had worked enthusiastically at creating a graphic look of white lettering on an orange and grey background that matched the eye-catching beach umbrellas, and coming up with graphically matched menu folders that proclaimed our customer promise:

FINE FOOD, FINE SURF, FINE TIMES

Over the previous 10 days, Sophie had devised with Chef Adith a simple menu of three starters, four main dishes and three desserts. They had decided the best approach was to do just a few dishes memorably with fresh ingredients.

The Spanish guests were volubly appreciative. Beginning with one of our three starters, 'fish-bites' (made like a Spanish croquette from flaked fish, herbs and mashed potato, then shallow pan-fried) served with spicy aioli, they followed them up with grilled super-sized jumbo prawns served with a combination of homemade Sri Lankan pickles and salad, then finishing with homemade coconut sorbet. All washed down with some chilled Chilean white wine

They complimented the chef, bringing Sophie and Adith out to meet them to lap up their accolades. Sophie smiled broadly, the ructions of the previous few days forgotten. Her food had won some hearts, and we'd gained some fans. And not just any old fans, but precisely the kind of guests we want to attract. The couple ran a small pensione in Madrid so they knew all about the importance of guest satisfaction.

They announced that the hotel's ambience was just right, 'It's so chic compared to where we've been staying,' and they wanted to move in immediately and stay for a week. After lunch, they took off to collect their bags, reappearing an hour later to check in.

Woohoo.

We have lift-off.

Chapter 15

FAULTY PALMS

It took some weeks before our barman Wasanta's fatal flaw emerged. It was tougher to resolve than the mistaken identity of the rats; through him we were introduced to the dark side of paradise.

When we had advertised for staff, he seemed an obvious choice: charming, knew how to mix a mean cocktail, and had worked in a cool bar nearby in the upmarket beach enclave of Unawatuna.

Mr Perfect.

But not everyone thought so. When Sophie was setting up the new kitchen with Chef Adith, she had much closer contact with both the kitchen and bar staff than we did. She grumbled about him. 'He's such a waste of space. Lazy and unhelpful. He's a real teenager, that one.'

In hindsight, this was an accurate assessment, but neither John nor I spotted any initial chinks in his charm. He was cool in his spotlessly clean AC/DC T-shirt and jeans, with his slicked back haircut – good looking, proactive to guests' needs and smooth.

The first warning light flashed a month after the hotel opened. Wasanta turned up at the hotel late at night with a thirty-something Finnish couple he introduced to us as his 'very, very good friends'.

The woman looked like the character Xena in the *Warrior Princess* TV series. Straight black hair, short stocky square body poured into a tiny, black-fringed skirt, and a black leather studded bra that barely contained an enormous bosom jutting out like a bathroom shelf. The look was finished off with lace-up Doc Martin boots. Eye-catching. With the constant threat of a studded nipple-gate, it wasn't the usual tropical beach-wear our other guests favoured.

She was over-the-top effusive on meeting us, grabbing and pushing me into her watermelon-sized breasts, while her dweeby-looking 'husband' pumped and pumped John's hand in some attempt at male bonding. Hyped up to the eyeballs on something, they went out to sit in the courtyard to drink (more?) vodka, with the diminutive Wasanta trailing in their wake.

'What on earth is the connection between them?' I wondered aloud. It didn't take long to find out.

A few days later, Wasanta didn't show up for his breakfast shift. Frantic to know if he was coming, John called his phone. Repeatedly.

No answer.

Just when the restaurant service was in full lunchtime swing and Latith was overwhelmed by the number of customers he had to serve, Wasanta ambled in.

'Where have you been?' John demanded.

'Ahhhh, sorry, Mr John, my mother is sick, and I have to take her medicine.'

We came to know this excuse as a version of 'the dog ate my homework', as sooner or later, all eight hotel staff, except for the chef, routinely had sick mothers or grandmothers. In some cases, the relative died, and a funeral ceremony erupted overnight that they had to attend the next day, meaning they wouldn't be coming into work. Sometimes the nominated person died more than once.

Late the following afternoon, Xena (as we called her) appeared back at the hotel, minus her husband, but in the same heavy metal outfit. She headed straight into the staff sleeping room – six bunk beds in one room next to the kitchen, where at least five of the staff slept overnight at any one time and napped during the day. I watched her warily. Instinct told me this was trouble, maybe big trouble coming.

'John, I think you need to sort this out. Wasanta can't invite Xena into the staff sleeping room. Why is she here when he's working? What's she up to?'

'No idea,' as he took off to find out.

'Wasanta, why is your friend in the staff room? She can't just come and wait there while you're working. Go and tell her she needs to come out. Right now... I want to speak to her.'

Xena started yelling obscenities from the staff room when Wasanta went in to find her. She emerged reluctantly.

As John began with, 'I don't want you...' she threw her arms into the air, her face contorted with rage.

'You, you can't tell me what to do,' she spat out. 'He is my friend. I come when I want. Anytime. You can't stop me.'

John was looming over her, talking in a low voice like a parent dealing with a tantrum-throwing toddler. He was trying not just to downplay the drama but switch it off.

Small groups of guests were sitting in our courtyard, sipping cocktails and watching as another blazing vermillion sun ball sank into the ocean, leaving the entire sky on fire with patches of hot orange and streaks of Schiaparelli pink with liquid gold reflected across the sea. Yet another psychedelic sunset. Happy hour underscored by the Cafe del Mar's chillout playlist in the background. And Xena screaming at John

'Okay, enough. I want you to leave. Right now.' John, in nightclub bouncer mode, was intimidating in his lowest vocal register. He towered over the top of her, drawing himself up to his full 190-centimetre height.

Xena stormed off, yelling, 'Fuck you, fat man.'

She turned back to face him when she reached the boundary strip of grass between our hotel and the beach, screaming, 'You fucking don't tell me what to do!' She stabbed the air with her pointed, black nail-polished index finger.

She turned her back to the hotel, faced the ocean; bent over, with her head between her legs, and flipped her skirt, mooning for all to see. The garden ground lighting illuminated her puckered anus, nestled between two white spheres.

I couldn't look at John, for fear of laughing.

Of all the impromptu performances at our Faulty Palms hotel, Xena's arse, silhouetted against the dazzling chocolate box sunset, was the *pièce de resistance*. The guests watched this unscheduled floor show in shocked silence, underscored by the cool lounge bar beats. John walked over to her and whispered that she was not to return to the hotel. Ever. If she did, he would call the police. She stormed off down the beach, yelling more obscenities, screaming that she would come back and that we'd be sorry; that she had friends.

Wasanta, having shrunk into the shadows behind the bar, shot off down the beach after her, leaving us one waiter down before the restaurant dinner service. He didn't return that night.

Vinod, stood impassively next to the bar watching. I went over. 'Vinod, what is going on with Wasanta?'

'Hmmm, I hear maybe some drug problem with Wasanta and his girlfriend,' he whispered out the side of his mouth.

Ahhhhh! So that was their connection.

This experience served as a wake-up call for us. Confirmation of the underbelly of 'paradise' in our village that I'd only heard passing reference to.

I knew how widespread marijuana was in grass and hashish form, but this was my first encounter with hard drugs.

According to Sri Lankan labour law, an employee has to be formally reprimanded three times before they can be sacked. Wasanta had been warned once over his 'sick mother' no-show, and now this was his second warning. John phoned Nalinda to tell him. But we had to sit on it until the next day, as he wasn't picking up his phone.

When he finally responded, Nalinda agreed to reprimand Wasanta formally but took John by surprise saying, 'I heard from a friend of mine that Wasanta was seen in Galle buying drugs. He is known to have that problem.'

'Why didn't you tell me this when we hired him six weeks ago?' John snapped.

'Because you wanted to hire him as a barman.' This answer only made things more confusing. Was Nalinda there to help us or trip us up? It was unclear.

Around 3 am, a drunk and crying Finnish 'husband' came barging past our beachside security guard to bang on the locked hotel doors. He was hunting for Xena, yelling out her name. Woken by the commotion and clad only in a sarong, John went down to tell him to go away, she wasn't there and he asked the security guy to escort him back to the beach.

At breakfast the next day, Vinod gleefully told me that the wailing husband found Wasanta and Xena passed out on some sun lounges in front of a hotel further down the beachfront. With his relish for gossip, he also revealed that they weren't married and the Finnish 'husband' paid Xena to come on holiday with him to Sri Lanka.

Xena made an encore appearance a couple of nights later, and it was even more spectacular than before.

Once again, right on sunset, she came up from the beach and stood on the hotel boundary grass strip, clutching a dog lead attached to an enormous black Doberman, a real hound of Hades. He was quite the accessory to the heavy metal black studded outfit she still wore.

Who knows where she found such a prop or to whom he belonged? I think she wanted to show us that she was one badass warrior woman not to be messed with. She was in complete Valkyrie vengeful flight mode or perhaps she believed she was channelling the Finnish goddess Loviatar, the muse of many heavy metal Finnish musicians, famous for turning into a shape-shifting witch at will.

Gripping the dog's collar, she yelled at the top of her voice, '*Nobody* tells me what to do. Nobody. And you,' pointing her free hand at John, chatting to guests in the middle of the courtyard, 'are just a big fucking iiiiidjiot.'

This was too much for John. He went straight inside and called Nalinda, who didn't answer. John asked Vinod to call the police, but they took so long to show up that Xena had long since scarpered off with her canine familiar. We never saw her again.

Wasanta didn't bother to show up for work. Again. When he did finally show, John served him with his third written warning and said he was sacked.

And with that, he vanished. We didn't see him again.

* * *

Just as the memory of Xena faded into the stories-to-dine-out-on category, a squad of Sinhalese yummy mummies from Colombo turned up early one Saturday morning. Five gorgeous, golden-limbed thirty-somethings disgorged from a fleet of chauffeured, late-model SUVs. Each woman came with a child, and each child had a nanny. This was to be the yummy mummies' girls-only weekend getaway. Slumming it in our racy surfside hipster village.

From behind the bar, Vinod watched them warily; Suresh and Jayantha lumbered across the courtyard under the weight of their luggage, taking their bags to each of the superior sea view rooms. The nannies were jammed into the cheap downstairs corridor rooms with their charges, two to a room.

'Ahhh, Colombo 7 ladies. Rich ladies,' Vinod sighed, with wry amusement glinting in his eyes.

Colombo 7 is the posh part of Colombo, home to gracious mansions, embassies, government ministers and five-star hotels. The suburb of choice for wealthy Colombo-ites.

Their demands came thick and fast.

'I need extra pillows.'

'Do you have pillows that are not so thick?'

'Give me extra towels.'

'I need you to replace the mosquito net in my room because there is a hole in it.'

'The air conditioning needs to be quieter.'

'The sea is thunderous; do you have earplugs?'

'We need a special rice and dahl menu for the children and the nannies. They will eat in the courtyard. Not the restaurant.'

Over the long weekend, the yummy mummies spoke only in English to us and each other. They told us proudly that they had gone to school and university in Australia. 'This is why we speak such good English.'

But all politesse was abandoned when each of the yummy mummies took turns standing in the hotel kitchen doorway barking orders in Sinhalese at the kitchen staff. No wonder Vinod sighed when they arrived. He knew what we didn't – that they would be our most demanding guests to date.

But John and I saw a potentially lucrative market if we got on the Colombo yummy mummy radar. I explained to the staff that they were our special guests and that no demand would be too much.

During the day, they lounged around in the hotel – gossiping, grazing the hotel's menu, drinking fresh juices, dipping themselves in the sea and lazing on the sun lounges. They were saving themselves up for their night-time forays. And how they dressed for the occasion! Competing for 'belle of the night' by pouring their beautiful, lissom bodies into strapless, tiny, figure-hugging, ruched-up tubes that barely grazed their nether regions, 'fanny covers' as John referred to their dress style of choice.

With his connoisseur's appreciation of female flesh, John watched them dance about the courtyard like exotic fireflies, downing cocktails at our bar before heading out down the dusty village road in their big city bright lights nightclub wear.

On their second night at our hotel, they were partying up a storm at happy hour, when our head housekeeper, Jayantha, pulled his most spectacular stunt. For which he remained remorseful for the rest of the time we were at the hotel.

John had tried to call him all afternoon after he hadn't returned from his parents-in-law's village. He'd promised us he'd be back early in the morning, but by late afternoon he still hadn't shown up. He wanted to have extra time off to visit his two children, who lived with his wife's parents because his wife worked as a housemaid in Dubai. Even though it was our busiest weekend we'd agreed because we saw how he visibly suffered from having his family split up, often seeing him on the beachfront at sunset, gazing sadly out to sea.

John repeatedly called him on Vinod's phone to try and get an answer. But no go.

Finally, like an apparition, he materialised right on happy hour.

The courtyard was crowded with the yummy mummies, other cocktail drinkers, buzzing conversations and the cool lounge music of India Arie playing. John went over and asked him where he had been.

Unwittingly, John set off some internal siren, and Jayantha started yelling in Sinhalese, 'This situation is impossible. I'm entitled to time off; no one understands my pain, and why am

I paid so little money anyway? I'm fed up. Absolutely fed up. I'm leaving this hotel. I'm leaving right now.'

The spotlight was now on him as the floor show; he was the centre of everyone's attention.

John could tell he was drunk. Very drunk. And that he needed to be removed, pronto.

'Vinod, please take Jayantha into the staff sleeping room. Now. And make sure he stays in there.'

While John went behind the bar to keep serving drinks to guests, Vinod led Jayantha off, still yelling, 'I'm going to resign; I've had it with this hotel and everyone here.'

After fifteen minutes, Vinod reappeared, telling John that Jayantha had passed out.

The yummy mummies watched this unscheduled show with sparkling eyes and little smiles at the corner of their mouths. Unlike us, they understood every word Jayantha said. We had to rely on Vinod's translation. To us, it was an impromptu cabaret performance of the worst kind. But when we went to apologise to our pride of princesses, they brushed it off.

'Ah, servants, they always make problems; what can you do?' putting their hands up in the air.

Some hours later, after dinner, Jayantha slunk back into the courtyard.

He apologised profusely several times over; he kept saying he didn't want to resign and was so sorry.

'Jayantha, this time, you've gone too far. We'll talk about it tomorrow,' John replied.

The following day, John formally cautioned him, stating that a three-strike rule was now in place. And that left two more strikes before he was out.

But for the moment, all was forgiven. Jayantha was back in the family.

The only other pastime on the yummy mummies' schedule was shopping. Not that Hikkaduwa afforded them quite the same range as in Colombo. But a seductive array of jewellery was available in the village shops, set in high-grade silver. Glittering gemstones of many sizes and varieties shone and sparkled in stores down the coast from Colombo to Galle. Just along the main road from our hotel was one called Super Jewels, which they all went to check out one afternoon. It more than lived up to its name.

One of the yummy mummies pranced back into the hotel courtyard with a crystal quartz pendant the size of a teacup saucer sitting mid-chest.

My eyes popped out, 'Is that cut glass?' I asked.

'Oh no, no, no,' she replied, shaking her head from side to side. 'This is *real* crystal quartz. Super Jewels is a government-certified shop. All real stones there.'

As her hand fluttered across the crystal plate protecting her golden-skinned cleavage housed only in a tiny singlet top, she told me about a present from her husband. 'He gave me a ring like Princess Diana's engagement ring, that now the Princess of Wales wears. A blue sapphire surrounded by diamonds. The sapphire came from Sri Lanka, you know. But I couldn't possibly wear my ring in a place like this.'

It made me wonder how many other replicas had been made in Sri Lanka of that very famous ring.

Sometimes, when I wanted a break from the hotel, I'd catch a tuk-tuk to the jewellery shops of Galle to gaze at their treasure trove. The jewellers were highly skilled in snaring female customers by playing up to their fascination with their stones. They could instantly assess the genuine buyers from the tyre kickers and gently press, corral and reel the buyer into a sale.

The most expert was the charming and courtly Mr Azziz in the Galle Fort's Dutch arcade Antiques and Stones shop. 'You know, Mrs Dasha, Sri Lanka has always been a mecca for semi-precious stones, long before the Portuguese arrived 500 years ago. Muslim gem merchants and stonecutters came to

Galle during the Crusades. They are my ancestors, my family. That's who I'm descended from. And my family still keeps our traditions; we close our shop every Friday at lunchtime to go to the mosque.'

There wasn't anything Mr Azziz didn't know about gemstones. He loved to talk about them; and to show me books about their mysterious talismanic properties, all the while bringing out tray after tray of exquisitely sumptuous unset stones. One day he decided that I must try on a very showy necklace made from rubies, emeralds, diamonds and sapphires that had just been completed for a customer.

'Just to see,' he said.

With a price tag of $US50,000, I was in little danger of making the purchase. But I did love looking at it around my neck.

I have long been fascinated with the power of precious stones; a fascination inherited from my mother. I understand why they have adorned men and women as talismans since people walked upright. Four months after arriving in Sri Lanka, I charged Mr Azziz with finding me a perfect aquamarine. It was strangely prophetic that I searched for this stone. 'You know, Mrs Dasha, the aquamarine's name is derived from Latin, meaning "water of the sea". They are beautiful crystals that heighten courage and aid clear communication with the divine source of all. These stones help build courage when handling grief and are powerful in assisting self-healing.'

How prescient his words would turn out to be.

The end of the long weekend of yummy mummies came, much to our staff's relief. We said our goodbyes to the sassy Colombo-ites and their retinues. While they haggled over their bills, they all said how welcome we made them feel.

The proof of this came two weekends later. One of the yummy mummies returned with a man who wasn't her husband, childless and paying cash.

John and I wondered how we could capitalise on this and turn it into a business opportunity; how to make our hotel the Colombo 7 destination for secret assignations?

* * *

Now that Nalinda was living offsite with his family, getting him to respond to day-to-day problems was becoming increasingly difficult. He was neither around nor involved when the crumbling hotel systems fell apart.

Some days after the yummy mummies left, the circuit breakers supplying the restaurant, kitchen, bar and garden lighting burnt out around 9pm at night. The main over-rider caught fire, and some cablings sparked and sizzled out in the roof. No lights, no power.

John and the night staff gathered around the blackened, smoking power board with torches, unwilling to touch it and unable to work out what had just happened.

John called Nalinda, 'I'm going to switch everything off until tomorrow. But we need the electrician to come first thing tomorrow morning. We've got no power. No power at all.' Nalinda said he'd call him.

No power meant no lights, only candles and oil lamps, no internet, no music and no way of making breakfast for a hotel full of guests.

John called the electrician early the following day but he knew nothing about the power board fire. Nalinda hadn't called him. But he came straight away to sort it out. Nalinda turned up after lunch saying, 'Big problem in the kitchen. Too many things taking power. Too many appliances.'

'But when the burn-out happened, the kitchen was closed. The problem is that the electrical wiring in the hotel is kaput.' John countered, 'You can't blame the increased occupancy and the hotel's success for the electrical circuit breakdown.'

Standing to the side, I watched a dark shadow of fury spread over Nalinda's face. He said nothing, turning to talk to the electrician in Sinhalese.

Later on, as John inspected some switches, I asked, 'Why is Nalinda so angry? Do you think you insulted him by saying the wiring he was responsible for installing was to blame for the supply problems?'

'Dunno. But wrangling Nalinda is turning into the most difficult part of this job. His lack of communication and disorganisation is starting to wear me down. Plus, it's clear he doesn't like us very much. I think he rather relishes being the only person who believes he knows how to keep this leaky boat afloat.'

'Maybe we should just call the hotel Faulty Palms?'

Bad timing, I realised, as soon as the words fell out of my mouth.

'Yeah, well, I'm no Basil Fawlty,' growled John, hunched over some switches on the hopefully restored circuit board.

The maintenance of paradise was getting more demanding. Certainly much trickier than we had ever imagined it would be. We knew before coming that the hotel was rundown, and it would be a challenge to bring it up to scratch. But now, with the dark underbelly we'd been introduced to and the faulty systems that were propping it up, the problems were looking insurmountable. The fantasy image of lounging casually under a palm tree in a hammock, sipping a pina colada with a paper umbrella stuck in a maraschino cherry was fading fast. If we'd ever had it in the first place

Chapter 16

NO. 3 HOTEL

'Mrs Dasha, Mrs Dasha, come quick. *Quick*. Turtle going to lay eggs.'

I zoomed onto the beach with Suresh, to watch the most wondrous ancient ritual take place. A giant green turtle hauling her 150 kilos out of the surf shallows up the beach. A long lumbering slide until she stopped halfway between our hotel and the shoreline. Slowly and rhythmically, she dug a shallow hole using her two back flippers, alternating between the left and right. She then pushed out a hundred and twenty rubbery, pearlescent spheres the size of an orange. It was late evening with a bright moon high in the sky and these spheres kept popping out for over an hour and a half.

We gave her a little privacy by turning off the front hotel beach lights, because she'd become a star attraction. From the moment she came out of the water, the village tom-tom started thumping up and down the beach – 'Turtle-turtle-turtle' – drawing a small crowd of locals and photo-snapping tourists around her. After using her flippers to cover her eggs with the sand she'd dug out before, she serenely slid back into the ocean, leaving her unhatched babies to an unknown fate.

While the turtle was laying her eggs, a khaki-clad member of the local tourist police raced down our hotel corridor and through the courtyard towards the beach, holding a gun in his outstretched hand with his pistol finger on the trigger. He was most definitely in the wrong movie. Who was he going to shoot? The turtle? Trailing in his wake were two other tourist police with, thankfully, holstered guns. It was surreal and inexplicable. Nobody called them, and no one knew why they came. In all the excitement over the popping eggs, they melted away just as soon as they arrived.

Suresh worried that the eggs were in immediate danger.

'Madame Dasha, we must call sea turtle hatchery in Habaraduwa. Right now. They must come and collect eggs.'

'Why?'

'Many men, they like to eat turtle eggs. People steal them to make money.'

Turns out that turtle egg omelettes are believed to enhance male virility. During the breeding season, poachers scan the beaches every night for any lucrative turtle egg action; then it's a race between the poachers, the tourist police and the hatchery workers as to who gets the eggs first.

We did call, but the hatchery said all their volunteers were busy doing other rescues and they'd get there when possible. Suresh and Latith stayed on egg guard for hours until they were collected, very gently, at 3am.

Turtles are a big deal in this part of the world; in popularity, size and number of species. In particular, the leatherback and green turtles. These ancient aquatic reptiles could always be relied upon to make an appearance to enthral our guests. At least three lived semi-permanently in the shallow reef up the beach from our hotel, and others came by to visit.

Sunset after sunset, our courtyard bar drew people together at Happy Hour, when we served half-price cocktails and vibed up the mood with a Salsa/Latino playlist.

John discovered a locally-brewed ginger beer, leading to the creation of the House Cocktail, the Surfside Special (based on a Moscow Mule): local vodka, fresh lime and ginger beer.

One evening, when a sandy-haired American marine biologist appeared, John told him the story of the turtle eggs and asked him, 'We've been told that turtles are hard-wired to go back to the beach they were born on, to lay their eggs. Is that true?'

He nodded, 'Yeah, it is.'

He had a different perspective on the two tourist turtle hatcheries that had sprung up nearby.

'I really wonder about the conservation benefits of these places. I worry that if turtles are born in captivity, the female turtle will not be stamped with the "magnetic imprint" of the beach she was born on, so she won't know where to return to lay her future eggs. Hatcheries work well as tourist attractions, where people can get up close and cuddle a baby turtle. But you'll find that many conservationists and scientists agree – it's much better to leave the eggs where they are hatched and to provide on-site protection so they remain unharmed. Then baby turtles can hatch naturally and make their way into the water.'

A noble ideal that ignores the lure of cash for predators who desperately need some.

* * *

Early morning. As the sun struggled to rise, the sticky humid air coated my skin, making me feel like I was covered in cling wrap. Pushing back the bed sheet, I nuzzled into John's sleeping back, my body spooning into his. As my nose pressed into his skin, my nostrils filled with an overpowering scent of cinnamon. Although not quite a turn-off, my sense of smell doesn't count it as an aphrodisiac. It has a staggering sweetness. Like being pressed up close to someone wearing too much aftershave in an elevator.

Sujith gave John a small bottle of cinnamon oil, telling him, 'This will fix bites and keep mosquitoes away.' From that moment, John overdosed on its application, convinced it was a one-stop remedy. Prevention and cure. Despite our queen-sized bed being swathed in a canopied tent of mosquito netting, mosquitoes never failed to find a way in to feast on his abundant flesh. In a biological quirk of fate, they found me inedible, ignoring me on their nightly ninja raids. The smell of cinnamon suffused our room, and our bed and hovered in my nostrils everywhere I went, permeating the humid air around me.

Sri Lankans cook with cinnamon, drink it in tea, or constantly daub themselves with its essential oil (extracted from the leaves) for any number of ills.

At an Ayurvedic treatment clinic down the road from our hotel, a practitioner told us that headaches, type 2 diabetes, arthritis, high blood pressure, high cholesterol, premature ejaculation and even cancer could all be treated with cinnamon oil. Not necessarily cured, but treated.

Curious to find out more about the source of this ever-present aroma, I persuaded John to come on a dawn expedition in search of cinnamon trees.

We set off in a narrow motorised canoe on the heart-stoppingly beautiful Madu River, heading to a cinnamon forest on one of the 25 islands in the river. Just as the sun rose, streaking the peacock blue sky in shades of pink and orange, the boatman told us at least 70 types of fish and 31 different kinds of reptiles could be found in this river. As we slid through mangrove tunnels, giant monitor lizards the size of crocodiles basked on rocks, keeping a lazy eye on us passing by. Eagles soared overhead, and beautiful kingfishers dive-bombed for fish. It was nature's dazzling Disneyland.

Stopping at one of the islands, we were taken to meet a weathered old cinnamon peeler named Vidurasena, sitting cross-legged, wearing a sarong and checked shirt, outside his mud-daubed house. Swiftly cutting off the outer layer of the stems of a cinnamon tree with a lethal-looking hooked blade, he removed the inner bark sheets, wrapping them around each other until he had a quill about 30 centimetres long. He stood up and slotted the quill in the strings of coir made from coconut fibre hanging beneath his coconut palm leaf roof, telling us they would be ready in eight days.

Once the quills had dried, he cut them into smaller lengths to be packaged up, or ground them to make the powdery cinnamon spice.

From the beginning of commercial navigation, cinnamon has always been Sri Lanka's most precious trading commodity. First the Romans, then the Arabs and the Chinese sailed to Sri Lanka (Galle and Jaffna were ports on the Silk Road Routes) to acquire it. Then the desire for ownership of the cinnamon trade drove the successive waves of colonisation from the Portuguese onwards.

I loved visiting the spice merchants in Galle; standing amongst the mounds of pungent-smelling powders spread out in open concrete-floored shops. Piles of cloves, cardamom, cinnamon, cumin, ginger, nutmeg, curry leaves, black peppercorns and red, red chillies. The symphony of smells was exhilarating. One of these spice merchants told me the most enchanting story.

'You know, in ancient times in Sri Lanka, the origin of cinnamon was kept a very deep secret. It was so valuable that the Arab traders invented amazing stories of giant birds who made their nests from the mysterious cinnamon sticks and guarded them, so that people had to risk their lives if they wanted to get the cinnamon.'

I loved this folktale and thought of it often as the fragrance of cinnamon grew on me more and more over time. When I inhaled directly from the tiny essential oil bottle, it brought on an immediate mood lift and instant relief from the 'pressure drop'.

Astonishingly, our dream of paradise was starting to come true. Languid days started rolling one into another, as the hotel settled into a laid-back tropical rhythm to the ambient Balearic beats on the playlists I created. Cool grooves like Ibiza's Café del Mar, Reggae and Dub music were the standout chill-out musical moods.

And the guests kept arriving in a steady stream via our website, word-of-mouth recommendations, or friends from Australia coming to check out our piece of paradise. Some were just walk-ins off the beach. Most of them were charming, amusing, and a pleasure to host, which resulted in guests writing up glowing Trip Advisor reviews.

John and I had rebranded the hotel by creating a pared-back, chic, boho/euro beachside style of cane furniture with orange accent furnishings set against white walls and polished concrete floors.

And it was paying off.

We stood out against the other mid-range hotels on the beachfront.

The large orange canvas umbrellas shadowing the sun lounges welcomed people into our courtyard. John loved playing the role of mine host, greeting guests, and ensuring they were well watered, fed and entertained. It was constant showtime for him, and he was the ringmaster taking people's money at the door.

When I first met John in the mid-1980s, he sported a business card proclaiming that he was a 'purveyor of fine entertainment and lowlife good times'. That impressed me.

In Sri Lanka, relaunching the hotel was his latest iteration of both.

The Mediterranean-Sri Lankan fusion dishes Sophie devised with our chef worked well with just a few minor tweaks. The menu showed off the coconut palm that reigns supreme in Sri Lankan cuisine. You can't have one without the other. The fruit of the Cocos Nucifera palm fringed all the beaches and was used in so many ways in our restaurant dishes. The coconut's white flesh was finely grated to make a moreish coconut chilli sambal to accompany curries, and in rotis to sop up the hodda (curry sauce) of spices infused in coconut milk, and the mallum salad was created by mixing fresh chopped leaves and coconut. Mixing grated coconut with water and pressing the mixture through a strainer made a thick milk extract used for cooking and dialling down hot curries.

Clear coconut oil, rich in saturated fats, was made from dried coconut and used as the principal cooking oil. We used jaggery syrup from the kithul palm tree flower to create our jaggery-flavoured ice cream.

Or we did when we could buy fresh cream. It was a scarce commodity and would appear, at best, once a week on the supermarket shelves when we would pounce and buy up the lot. Aerosol cream could be sourced everywhere but made terrible fake ice cream that wouldn't set properly.

Our hotel bar sold an 'aged' five-year-old arrack, a traditional and lethal Sri Lankan white spirit distilled from the fermented sap of unopened coconut flowers. A single coconut palm tree can yield up to two litres of arrack daily, so it was understandable that it was the standard drink of choice. Cheap, plentiful and sometimes up to 90% proof.

A young Australian girl, Sri Lankan born, arrived to stay with her adoptive mother and a surfboard. She came looking for her birth mother. A Sri Lankan Tamil guest talked with her and later told me, 'I'm sure this girl is a Tamil because of her look and facial features.'

She never did find her birth mother or any details of her birth. It was most often Tamil children who were the collateral damage of the civil war, either orphaned and put up for international adoption, or offered up by living families whose lives had been destroyed and saw no option but to adopt them out. But no records could be found post-war to give any clues. All of them were destroyed or never kept in the first place.

Other situations called for celebration. An uber-attractive-looking young couple, an Englishman and an Australian, popped up one afternoon. A mutual friend recommended they stay at our hotel; they turned out to be the rising British movie star Ben Whishaw and his now former husband, Mark Bradshaw. Having established the connection, John invited them to his evening birthday dinner that night. He planned it as a celebration for everyone to share and as a champion excuse for a fireworks display.

John always ensured that he was the centre of attention on his birthday. And this Sri Lankan one was a unique occasion to draw old friends who had come to visit us in the hotel, new friends and anyone else he thought would be fun to join in the party and watch his prized fireworks light up the sky.

In the afternoon, John headed off to set up the fireworks canisters with the fireworks maestro on the beach in front of the hotel for this birthday extravaganza. With just an hour before our guests arrived for dinner, we kept our fingers crossed that the electrics would hold out for the evening.

We also experienced romance with a capital R in the air. When an English couple announced their engagement at our bar one night, the champagne, or what passed for it, popped around the bar.

Sourcing alcohol from the local bottle shop was something of a lucky dip, and had its pitfalls. Counterintuitively, we never bought wine that was older than a couple of years' vintage, sourced from Chile, South Africa, Australia, and Italy. We discovered from experience and other expats' stories that wine's importation was haphazard when it came to the use of refrigeration. It wasn't unknown for some wine shipments to sit for days, if not longer, unrefrigerated in the blazing tropical heat, causing them to turn a much darker than intended colour, on occasion validating the venerable Aussie expression, 'Tastes like cat's piss.'

As the days passed serenely in a frangipani-scented heat haze of beachside bonhomie to laid-back reggae beats, behind the scenes it was a constant battle to keep the leaky boat of a hotel afloat.

Most days, the power would cut out. Perhaps for an hour. Maybe four hours. Sometimes longer. No power meant no fans, no air-conditioning, no refrigeration in the bar and kitchen, no internet and a lot of exasperated guests we had to schmooze and soothe.

Infuriatingly, at times, it was only our hotel that went down while the other surrounding places were powered up. It was impossible to predict when it might happen, and Nalinda insisted it wasn't necessary to buy a backup generator. Instead, the staff would raise their hands, palms upward, saying, 'What to do?'

It became apparent that the hotel's power circuits were not coping, as the electrical systems kept breaking down, with electric shocks still coming off light switches when we touched them. Nalinda's friend, the electrician, looked nonplussed every time there was a new problem. Even when a small fire caused by faulty wiring broke out in the roof, he remained impassive and imperturbable.

One morning, the downstairs water supply went out. Just stopped. Dead. Not a drop out of any of the taps. Nalinda was nowhere to be seen, so we asked our head housekeeper, Jayantha, if he knew anything about the water pump system.

'Yes,' he said.

He went with John into the front garden to find the pumphouse box. Sitting on his haunches in front of it, he fiddled with the taps, and the water burst back on, throwing Jayantha backwards, dazed and groaning in pain. He rolled onto his front, vomited, and kept saying, 'My arm, my arm, can't feel anything,' clutching it in front of him.

We tried to help him stand, but it took at least fifteen minutes for him to be able to get to his feet. He'd suffered a massive electric shock from the bare wires inserted into the pump. Wires that were not encased in any plug to protect them. Or anyone touching them.

'John, he could have been killed. Jayantha has to go to the hospital. Now. You call Nalinda. See if he'll take him.'

Thankfully, Nalinda answered. A short staccato conversation went to and fro.

John turned to me, 'Nalinda says Jayantha can't go to the public hospital because it'll make big trouble. I'm not sure if that's because he's working illegally for us, or maybe it would be big trouble for the hotel. One of the boys needs to take him to a private doctor in a tuk-tuk, and we'll pay.' Jayantha was a sad-eyed ex-Sri Lankan Army soldier injured in a skirmish during the civil war. Because of his ongoing injuries, he received a tiny armed services pension that was not enough for his family to live on.

He texted John the next day, saying that although the ECG test didn't reveal any problem, his arm was still sore and not working so well. Three days later, he returned, saying his arm was fine.

Escalating emails were sent by John to Nalinda, trying to keep the hotel afloat. With increasingly long lists of maintenance required, John's anguish level rose with each email.

I remonstrated with him over what I felt was his snippy email tone. I told him I thought he was being insensitive towards Nalinda.

But he was unapologetic.

'Fuck it! We're trying to run a business, and Nalinda's not keeping his end of the deal. Nick says he has to handle all the maintenance problems. But we're drowning in them!'

John was clearly losing patience, not the time to talk him down with sweet talk.

Despite the almost daily Faulty Palms breakdowns, the hotel was humming along on a successful groove we had set.

Just four months into running the hotel, we were beyond thrilled to read that Trip Advisor ranked us number three hotel on the beach and number five out of 22 hotels in Hikkaduwa.

This was huge for us.

Not bad, we told ourselves, for a hotel that was completely off the radar and had only negative reviews four months ago.

This was the tangible payoff for all our hard work. We had taken the hotel from off the radar to rave reviews, which emboldened us to keep doing what we were doing.

The hotel's continuing success meant that we were now feeding and housing up to 40 people a day, smoothly and efficiently, or so it appeared to them.

One spasm in the hotel works involved the hotel's laundry service provider, who in turn provided me with a valuable, although rather painful lesson.

I had bought beautiful soft white towels for the hotel and had sent them off to be washed by a new laundry service. They were returned stained, tatty, old and scratchy.

'These are not our towels.'''

'This ones your towels, Madame. These towels you give me.'

'No, they're not. They're just not. I want our towels back. Now.'

With his chin jutting out and eyes blank, the laundryman stood impassively in front of me like an Easter Island statue. 'No, Madame, these towels belong this hotel, these towels you give me.'

No amount of confrontation, raised angry voices (mine), or threats of going to the police (John) succeeded in recovering our 30 brand-new, fluffy white towels. Gone. Vanished. Pfffff. Just like that.

My angry arguing, hopping from foot to foot, did not change this outcome.

Whatsoever.

Nalinda was called to mediate in Sinhalese, but stood off to one side watching, declining to intercede. Then he pointed at me, saying in English, 'If you wrote name of hotel in black pen on towels, this not happen.'

I understood that he was signalling to the laundry man that my behaviour was a white lady's problem. Not his. I had committed the cardinal behavioural sin in Southern Asia. I lost my cool. And behaved like a hated white Madam.

Nalinda wasn't about to align himself with me against a Sri Lankan man. We never did get our brand-new fluffy white towels back again.

But after the Trip Advisor reviews went online praising John and me by name as the perfect hosts, claiming the food was delicious, and its recent refurbishment made it the most attractive hotel on the strip, it was a total punch-the-air moment.

Sri Lanka's least experienced hoteliers had pulled it off!

For now.

Chapter 17

THE BARMY ARMY

Christmas is coming when the Barmy Army invades.

A group of 16 extended family and friends arrived from Essex, pre-booking 12 of our 15 rooms. Led by a peroxided alpha female, Gemma, they were the live version of the reality TV series, *The Only Way Is Essex*.

They went on to prove they could out-bling, out-drink, out-dance and shout louder than all the other guests we'd had to date. But, from day one, they made it clear that they'd insist on value for money. Or their concept of it.

'Dasha, I need a new toilet seat,' Gemma demanded an hour after arriving. 'Mine is way too small, and it's giving me a black man's pinch.'

Whoa, I was utterly blindsided hearing this phrase. Not only had I never heard it before, but hearing it used in Sri Lanka? Turns out it's a derogatory term for a blood blister.

But was she for real?

This was a real gotcha moment for me because, as the host, no comment about whether it was appropriate was warranted, but it made me deeply uncomfortable.

'Okay, I'll look into it,' was all I could think to reply. I arranged for a handyman to exchange Gemma's toilet seat with one of the restaurant toilet seats. A deft solution to the problem, or so I thought.

Not in her eyes.

'Well, now I can't use that one because I'll have the same problem,' Gemma sniped.

'It's the best I can do right now,' I replied, hoping she'd forget about it.

The Essex clan stayed for two noisy weeks, amusing us all with their tribal antics. Made up of husbands, wives, mothers, fathers, sons, daughters, girlfriends, boyfriends and a couple of ring-ins, they were all practised in the art of holidaying together, bringing a variety of party props. Gemma and her sister appeared at breakfast one morning, wearing white bikinis, matching blow-up plastic yellow wigs with purple crowns and clutching blow-up wands that make them look like a pair of life-sized fairground kewpie dolls. They performed a little 'boop-boop-y-do' song together, and the group laughed raucously.

The clan's tourist sightseeing was mainly of the nocturnal variety, going from bar to bar, engaging in nightly drinking competitions, dancing on tables and getting hammered on the local lethal cocktails. Their days were spent on the hotel's sun lounges, recuperating from the previous night and boasting about who got the drunkest. All this while working their hardest to get a suntan, a shade of colour the French refer to as *rostbif* when describing the English in the sun.

Early evening, they would regroup to take advantage of our happy hour cocktail prices.

Showered, primped and perfumed, particularly the men, their dress code could be described as smart-casual cocktail wear. The women sparkled and shone, showing off expensive jewellery, scores of sequins and oiled skin, while the men dressed ready to prowl.

Their favourite night-time haunt was Ranjith's beach hut bar, 300 metres down the shoreline.

John referred to it as 'The Bar at the End of the Universe', with its chipped walls with leftover 1970's murals, graffiti and a blaring jukebox in a brutalist concrete shell. Business was booming for the jovial, well-connected and prosperous Sinhalese owner. Surfies, backpackers and aged Euro hippies (some left over from the early 1970's hippie invasion themselves) gather, dancing, drinking, and smoking weed.

There was no set closing time. Night after night, the Essex pack shouted, sang and danced on the tables, drinking their collective weight in arrack. The bar owner loved them. And they loved him right back.

But Gemma of Essex displayed definite boundaries when it came to parties she wasn't invited to.

An escalating problem had developed in our next-door neighbour hotel. When the hotel failed to attract overnight guests, the beach boys staff hit on a financial rescue plan so they could get paid.

A weekly, all-night dance party.

They set up a couple of turntables on a rickety table outside facing the beach with giant speakers right next to our shared courtyard wall. To create a makeshift club area, they hoisted some bamboo poles sunk into the sand and strung up a couple of fishermen's nets.

Abracadabra – an instant party zone that funnels people through a narrow opening with an entrance fee.

Wednesday nights turned into a very loud doof-doof zone with bad, un-danceable, local reggae music blasting the night with the volume cranked up so high the speakers muffled and crackled.

The week before Christmas, the weekly party was raging when Gemma, the Boudicca of Essex, came into her own. Fed up with being unable to sleep, she stormed next door at 4am, ripped out the power cords, threw over a chair and screamed at the drunken DJ, who'd collapsed over the decks, 'This party is *over*.'

I secretly cheered.

But every Wednesday, we saw the handwritten sandwich board impaled into the beachfront next door announcing:

Party in Hotel Tonite

DJ MUSIC UNTIL SUNRISE

We shuddered and fretted. It was a threat to our business.

Guests grizzled, complaining loudly about the noise bleeding into our premium suites. John's great friend of 25 years, broadcaster Wendy Harmer, visited us with her family for a quiet surfing holiday. Instead she ended up curled on the bathroom floor, jammed between the basin and the toilet, with a pillow wedged over her head, trying to block out the noise.

The following day, she greeted John and me with, 'That was the worst night of my life.'

Wendy went off to a nice hotel in Galle to recuperate. Something had to give.

Working out what to do about it turned out not to be easy. Beachside nightlife, we discovered, was unregulated, and despite Gemma's dramatic intervention, the next-door parties continued. We could only think that permission relied on how much was paid to whom to have what you wanted. There certainly was no one or nowhere we could complain. The tourist police station down the beach turned a blind ear.

There were notional time limits on loud noise at night, but no one seemed to enforce them. Nalinda and Nick tried to talk to the absent owners of the next-door hotel. But no go. The music raged on through blown speakers once a week for six weeks. Then, in the seventh week, The Party Was Over. Finished.

No more doof-doof.

No one could or would say why. It just was. We breathed a deep sigh of relief.

With Nalinda living off-site, he had made it very clear that he didn't want to get involved with the hotel next door over their doof-doof parties, whether through indifference to our problem or fear of who he would be dealing with.

He didn't elaborate.

Although the beach parties finished, the dramas with the Essex tribe continued. A couple of days later, Gemma was in a state.

'Dasha, you have to do something! The security guard looked in my and my daughter's windows when we were in the bathroom. He watched as I put cream all over my *naked* body!'

I hastily fixed white A4 paper sheets over the clear glass panes with sticky tape while John said he would speak to the guards. They looked at him blankly, pretending not to understand English.

Like all the hotels along the beachfront during the tourist season, we had two security guards who came on at sunset and stayed until dawn. One sat at the front of the hotel, the other at the back of the hotel on the beach side. Security guards were predominantly former members of the Sri Lankan Army, who, after the civil war was over, had no other skill set or job prospects.

While standing or sitting on guard was something they knew how to do, they were not without their problems. One night a fight broke out at 3am – between our two guards! On his hourly inspection, the front guard found the back guard fast asleep in a chair, so he broke an empty beer bottle over his head. Standing in just my sarong alongside John, trying to calm them down, it seemed comical that now we were guarding the guards against each other.

There was only one time the Essex clan left Hikkaduwa's bars and our beachfront in the two weeks they stayed at our hotel. They went on a whale-watching safari boat trip off the coast near Mirissa.

By all accounts, it was not a raging success. Heavily hungover from the night before, most of them got seasick on the Sri Lankan Navy-operated boat trip, and no whales bothered to show, which was not an infrequent tourist complaint. Despite the whale trip brochures showing breaching whales cavorting in large numbers, paying $90 a head didn't guarantee a sighting.

While they were out whale hunting, I walked past Vinod leaning on the front of the small outdoor bar as he whispered sideways at me, 'Mrs. Dasha, Mrs Dasha, you see that one old German tourist lady? She is 70 year old and has a 27-year-old Sri Lankan boyfriend,' he nodded at the beachfront. I saw a tall, ancient, bikini-encased woman walking by with long grey seaweed hair. Almost skeletal, her skin hung off her in elephant folds.

'Lucky her,' I quipped.

'Nooo... Mrs. Dasha. Lucky him. He maybe get visa to go to Germany. Get good job. Send money back to his family.'

Vinod thought this was a good deal for both of them. His large round dancing eyes always glinted with amusement at what he saw around him. Intelligent and quick-witted, he loved gossip and was an endless source of information about the passing parade in front of and around the hotel.

It wasn't hard to pick out the beach boys sitting in front of our hotel. Aged anywhere from 16 to 30, they sat in groups of twos or threes, constantly shirtless, parading their buffed bodies, bedecked in silver chains and necklets; many with blonde hair tips. They plied their sex wares to any woman on a tourist visa, regardless of shape, age or nationality. Romance in paradise was an everyday commodity on our beachfront, alongside surf lessons, snorkelling and massage.

Most of the hotels, including ours when we arrived, displayed signs saying:

NOT ALLOWED TO ENTERTAIN BEACH BOYS IN ROOMS

Although there was a local laissez-faire attitude to this kind of male sex work, it jangled the Buddhist mores of the local community, as did the habit of tourists wearing only bikinis when wandering along the busy main Galle Road in front of the shops and snack spots. Pretty soon, there were street signs, in English and Russian, showing a red encircled white-painted male in a swimsuit and a white female figure in a bikini with a red ban line through them. English and Russian words, in capitals, were written underneath:

SWIMMING SUITS ONLY ALLOWED AT BEACH.

The beach in front of the hotel was a daily parade of people and tableaux. Russian girls in tiny bikinis, wearing thong bottoms (the kind that Brazilians called dental floss) with overly enhanced breasts, prancing along the shoreline for their boyfriend's video, imitating some Versace advertisement.

Sinhalese beach sellers, mainly women, ploughed up and down the beach in the scorching midday sun while carrying enormous bags of sarongs and bedspreads on their heads. The widow Sandemale came by every day selling sarongs, cheap shirts, sundresses and small animals made of shells, calling out, 'You buy, you buy? 'She dragged her prosthetic leg – the result of a train accident – through the burning sand to haggle with tourists over 50 cents when they spent four times that on a beer.

A charismatic, slender man with piercing hazel eyes and aquiline features came by most days with a massive, pale-coloured python draped around his neck like a living scarf. Sidling up to female tourists on the beach with the snake's head gripped in his hand, he would stroke his cheek with the snake and offer photo opportunities. Most women resisted. We were told that there was an encampment of beach gypsies, known as Telugus, further up the coast where he came from.

Sri Lankan Telugus were thought to have come originally from India and were seen as outcasts and trespassers. They relied on training snakes and monkeys and telling fortunes to make their living.

Vinod was very dismissive of the snake charmer, warning us not to encourage him because he was 'a bad man'.

Not that he could, or would, say what was bad about him.

The Barmy Army was gearing up, and preparations were underway for Christmas the next day. Christmas dinner in our restaurant was sold out; traditional Sri Lankan musicians were booked to come and play, and Chef was excited. A very tall pine-like tree was found and decorated with paper stars, handmade by local children who attended a nearby community centre that teaches traditional dance. This centre was set up as a post-tsunami exercise in community rebuilding and was run by an enterprising 70-year-old volunteer English woman called Eddi and her spaniel dog, Zigger.

Eddi kept us apprised of local gossip and local superstitious undercurrents. She sent us an email on Christmas Eve warning that the local community claimed the end of the world was foretold in the Mayan Calendar, which is why the tourists weren't coming.

Tourist numbers were indeed a little depleted that month.

Christmas night, the restaurant was full, feasting on a special Sri Lankan curry buffet that Chef created. The music was pumping, and the festive mood was infectious. The wine flowed. I looked around at one point to see John twirling Gemma of Essex on the improvised dance floor, laughing as they spun around. Everybody was happy, imbued with the Christmas spirit.

Chapter 18

HAPPY NEW YEAR

The day after Christmas, we flew off to the neighbouring Maldives for four days. This was not a holiday we'd planned to take, but a necessity to legalise our residential status in Sri Lanka.

Three weeks before, John had laid down an ultimatum to Nick. We were having trouble getting business visas despite Nick's promises of high-placed contacts who could seal the deal for us. After three months of working illegally on tourist visas, John lost patience.

'If our business visas are not issued now, Dasha and I will be forced to leave on 31 December.'

It worked.

We handed over our passports to a local fixer in his sprawling Galle Fort office and within days, our passports were stamped with the prized business visas.

At last, we were legal.

But there was one catch. We had to leave Sri Lanka and re-enter the country to activate them.

Exhausted and frayed from months of working 14 to 16-hour days, we needed to recharge and a few days in the nearby Maldives seemed a great choice. An island country of coral atolls promising snorkelling and lazing in the sun, the online brochures promoted it as a romantic honeymoon destination. And we certainly needed a few days of romance.

However, the island we chose because of its low cost, Thulusdhoo, didn't live up to the brochures' promises, with very basic accommodation, sewage running out of a pipe into the sea, and strictly enforced Islamic dress code, which made swimming forbidden and lazing in the sun impossible. Still, it was a welcome opportunity to luxuriate in each other's company without the competing demands of a busy hotel. The island's single claim to fame was that it was the only Coca-Cola bottling plant in the sub-continent to use desalinated water.

After the austere Islamic culture of our barren Maldives island, it was a relief to land back amongst the familiar frenetic chaos of Colombo's traffic. As we headed back to Hikkaduwa, a tuk-tuk cut across in front of our car, flashing a slogan from the back of its roof canopy that made me laugh:

YOU CAN'T MIX YOUR COCONUTS

Arriving back at the hotel that afternoon, there was palpable tension in the air, with limited eye contact between us and anyone else. While we were away, Nick, who was visiting on holiday from the UK and Nalinda had managed the hotel together. It had been hectic and demanding; for Nalinda, it was just like the good old days when he was running the hotel.

When he was in charge.

It was December 30th, and some restaurant staff worried there weren't enough bookings for the New Year's Eve dinner.

All along the beachfront, New Year's Eve celebrations were a big deal in Hikkaduwa. The hotels, guesthouses and bars competed to outdo each other with fireworks displays. It was an annual tradition in our hotel.

But the big difference this year was that Nalinda wasn't organising ours. His glowering eyes followed us all the following afternoon as we set up the restaurant for New Year's Eve.

In an attempt to include Nalinda in the celebrations, John suggested to him that he set up the barbecue and cook grilled fish on the night to complement the food Chef was preparing. While Suresh and Vinod set up an old half-44-gallon drum on a steel frame with a makeshift grill, I watched Nalinda as he looked on, smoking, slowly clenching and releasing his fist.

John's way of dealing with Nalinda's obvious discomfort was to focus on setting up the fireworks display on the beach, working with the local fireworks' maestro to make it happen. He was in firework heaven, with a rich choice available and cheap to purchase. It was the live ephemeral show John adored above all others, featuring his favourite things in life – colour, fire, excitement and controlled danger.

The next day was New Year's Eve. Around 30 guests bought tickets for dinner, and Chef had outdone himself with the range of food planned. It was to be a buffet-style meal of Sri Lankan curries, with special decorations for the table. Chef had carved beautiful table lanterns out of watermelons, a gesture of goodwill and well-meaning above all else.

Nalinda was late in setting up the barbecue, which made John worry that the fire wouldn't be hot enough to cook the fish in time to serve with the other dishes that Chef had prepared.

Sure enough, there was a timing screw-up, so the grilled fish and prawns were offered as a 'second' main course long after the other food had been served.

One of the guests brought his plate over to John, complaining that the fish wasn't cooked. John took it over to Nalinda, standing at the barbecue with his electrician friend. 'Do you think we can cook this one a bit more? The guest says it's underdone.' Nalinda looked at him, took the fish and said nothing. Next thing, Nick shot across the courtyard, highly agitated.

'What did you say to Nalinda? He's very, very upset. He says you have insulted him. In front of his friend. You're going to have to apologise.'

I could see the muscles tighten in Nick's neck. John attempted to explain.

'All I said was that the fish wasn't cooked properly. And it wasn't. He set up too late, and this is the result. He's also been drinking. Probably why he's so angry.'

But Nick wasn't buying it. 'You've offended him. You have to do something.'

'No, I'm not going to apologise. Nothing to apologise for. You know why he's behaving like this,' said John, leaving his words dangling in the air.

Nick walked off, his forehead scrunched into a frown and his jaw clenched. Nalinda was now challenging John out in the open, and getting Nick into the act. It felt like something new was going seriously awry.

As the sky lit up above us with a succession of gold and silver bursts of stars and the guests wrote their names in the air with sparklers, I caught sight of Nalinda's face as he stood off to the side with his friend.

In the exaggerated light of the fireworks, his eyes seemed to bulge in anger, and his face glowered.

The dance music cranked up, but my feet wouldn't move; I couldn't feel the beat. I was anxious, dislocated and uncomfortable. All the bonhomie of the night had evaporated like smoke. And I didn't know how to snatch it back. Neither Nalinda nor Nick spoke to John or me again that night, not even at midnight, to wish us a Happy New Year.

Tension was escalating with no obvious way of heading it off.

Chapter 19

GLOVES OFF

It didn't take much longer for it to bust out into the open.

The more successful the hotel became, the surlier, more unhelpful, and more obstructionist Nalinda became.

But it took a meeting with the accountant Mr Gopal, Nick and Nalinda just after New Year's Eve to demonstrate the depth of Nalinda's enmity.

Arriving in a late model corporate-looking car, Mr. Gopal epitomised 'Colombo money'; sleek, plump and with the patina of prosperity, he was a Colombo dude dressed in sharp business clothes with an open-necked long-sleeved shirt, his only concession to beach wear.

We all sat down together to get a clear picture of what the capital expenditure had been to date on refurbishing the hotel and calculating the hotel's total income and outgoings according to invoices and receipts.

When we had arrived as managers, the hotel relied on an antiquated, manual account-keeping system. Nalinda, as the bookkeeper, wrote up the receipts in a large exercise book. Guests were given hand-written carbon copy invoices to pay cash at the end of their stay. There was no form of a computer system in place to keep track of expenditure. John and I collected monies owed from guests, then wrote up the amounts in a small lined schoolbook and deposited the money in the hotel's safe. Once a week, Nalinda collected the accumulated cash from the safe and took it to the bank. No credit card payment system was in place, although it had been promised.

The only system that operated in the bar and restaurant was staff memory. They would write down, as they went, what the guests consumed.

Rubbery, to say the least. At best, the system was fluid; at worst, subject to manipulation.

Despite our insistence on wanting to change to a digital bookkeeping system, it never happened. Paper was how it was done. And how it would continue.

The meeting commenced with us seated around a long rectangular table. I immediately sensed unease as John and I sat facing Gopal, Nalinda and Nick. The seating alone made it look like 'us versus them'.

Nick began the conversation by explaining that the expenditure did not match the receipts and invoices. There was a shortfall. Money was missing.

My heart plunged to the pit of my stomach. *What's he saying? Is he suggesting that we are responsible for the missing money? Is this for real?*

As these thoughts raced through my mind, I sensed that beside me, John felt the same. He asked in a measured, neutral tone, 'Have *all* the invoices been counted that we gave to Nalinda? Including the ones we gave him two days ago?'

John stood up and pointed across the table to a folder in front of Nalinda. 'Those, in that batch? Have you counted those and included them in your calculations?' He sat down, his body stiffening, his fingers curling into fists beside me.

Gopal flicked through the invoices in the folder, one by one, while speedily adding them up on his calculator. Clickety-clack. Clickety-clack. 'Ahhh... yes, now it all adds up. Those invoices make up the gap.'

The meeting ended shortly after in a bit of a blur.

John and I were utterly blindsided and went outside for a nervous cigarette together. 'Did Nick and Nalinda just insinuate that we had stolen money? Or am I paranoid?'

'Nope. That's precisely what happened. The gloves are off. Nalinda's playing dirty. It's pretty clear he's trying his utmost to get rid of us, wouldn't you say?'

I looked at John with my stomach heaving like an acid bath. 'You think so...?' My words trailed off.

* * *

The meeting unnerved me. I could feel a dark, brooding treacherous undercurrent, seething with suspicion and jealousy swirling around us, undermining all the goodwill we had achieved in our little patch of paradise. The traditional Sri Lankan beliefs in spirits, magic and demons hovered over and all around us.

In a small mask museum near Ambalangoda, a beautiful, somewhat aloof guide, tightly wrapped in a figure-hugging silk sari, showed us the carved and painted medicine masks on the walls. She explained how in a Sanni exorcism ceremony, the shamans or medicine men who wore the traditional carved wooden devil masks performed *yakuma* – invocations to devils – to drive out illnesses or curse enemies. She showed us the group of 18 Sanni devil masks with their disfigured, discoloured faces and leery, bulging eyes. They were worn in ceremonies to drive out illnesses ranging from cholera, migraine, madness, gastro illness, fever to deafness.

I was fascinated by the power of belief in these masks and visited the museum on numerous occasions. But when I asked if they are still used in exorcism ceremonies, I was met with evasiveness: 'Well, yes, they are. Some people believe in magic.'

'Do you know how I can see one of these ceremonies?' I asked.

'Ahhh, no. I don't know where they are. But you can buy this book about the masks for 500 rupees.' She lifted a copy, signalling the conversation was over.

After one museum visit, John and I drove back to the hotel along the coastal road, passing buildings destroyed in the tsunami that had never been rebuilt. I turned to John, 'Do you think these spirits and demons are part of the tension and fear beneath the surface here?'

'I think we're seeing the other side of the "ideal tourist destination". Sri Lanka is beautiful. Tropical, Buddhist, a palm-fringed paradise with kind, happy, friendly people. No question. But that's not all it is.'

To the tourist's eye, Sri Lanka is the most pristine, sultry, and as yet undeveloped paradise on earth. But as with any paradise, there is always a serpent ready to strike in the Garden of Eden.

Over the time we spent in Sri Lanka, we saw how 26 years of ruthless civil war had decimated this Garden of Eden, leaving it psychologically pockmarked.

The war ended in 2009 in a final bloody massacre, when the defence minister Gotabaya Rajapaksa ordered the Sri Lankan army to attack an estimated 40,000 non-combatant Tamils, including women and children. The final confrontation took place on a north-eastern beach at Mullivaikkal when civilians along with the remaining renegade Tamil Tiger force were killed by Sri Lankan ground and airborne forces.

We saw first-hand through neighbours and staff how the devastating impact of the Sri Lankan Government's wars against the Liberation Tigers of Tamil Eelam in the north, and Maoist leftist insurgents in the south, during the 1980s and 1990s had deeply scarred the psyche of people we knew.

It was clear to us that this war damaged a whole generation, creating a country that was suffering extreme post-traumatic stress, with people inured to hatred and violence. When the war concluded, an estimated 100,000 Sri Lankans had been killed.

Unwatched by the rest of the world, this war raged for three decades, leaving everyone affected by the loss of family members and the lingering physical and psychological injuries. Shocking reports of extreme brutalism surfaced; not just dead bodies, but sightings of severed heads impaled on spikes in villages in the south.

No side was blameless; all parties in the civil war perpetrated atrocities. And although a United Nations report in 2011 accused the Sri Lankan Government of war crimes, more than a decade later, no one has been called to account.

Our head housekeeper, Jayantha, had his leg calf severely damaged by shrapnel in a civil war skirmish, leaving him with terrible scarring and a bad limp. He served in the Sri Lankan Army up north, not far from Jaffna, where his platoon was ambushed by the Liberation Tigers of Tamil Eelam (LTTE). The Tigers were a fearsome fighting force that wore cyanide capsules around their necks called *kuppies*, so they could suicide rather than be captured. Jayantha saw half of his platoon wiped out in front of him. This was why he was retired on a small army pension.

When John organised his big firework displays at our numerous hotel celebrations, Jayantha, on hearing the whistle of the firework's rockets as they were taking off, would dive down, yelling, 'Everyone hit the ground!'

It was never clear whether it was a joke, but the haunted look in his eyes and the panic on his face was very real.

As I watched the rockets explode into iridescent showers on the night of John's birthday, I wondered if it was the Sri Lankan spirit world pushing us around.

I could feel the force of Nalinda's jealousy all around us, threatening some unknown maelstrom.

* * *

We knew we had to talk with Nick to get some things straightened out. After the drama of New Year's Eve, and then the meeting with the accountant, we needed to know where we stood. We told him that Nalinda was continually obstructing us, didn't listen to us when we asked him to do things for the hotel, and refused to do even the most basic of maintenance that the hotel needed. Nick's response confirmed what we were thinking, but didn't want to believe.

'I've told him that he has to cooperate with you, but he says he hates you. Both of you. Because of what you are doing in the hotel. He won't say it's because the hotel is successful and you're showing him up. Instead, he's saying he hates the food you're serving and the staff you hired because they don't respect him. So yes, you're not imagining it; there is a problem between you and Nalinda. A big problem.'

I wondered if Nick was being straight with us. For the first time. Had he ever actually told Nalinda that he was bringing us in to replace him?

Something wasn't adding up. Nalinda's animosity towards us seemed way out of proportion. But I couldn't put my finger on it, nor find the words to ask Nick the question.

Nick's gaze shifted from us out towards the ocean. John and I looked at each other with a 'so we haven't been imagining it' look.

I made a faint sound while lifting my chin, 'Ahhhhhh, okayyy'.

The discussion had reached an awkward standstill, and Nick went off for a surf, saying we'd regroup later to work out how to deal with the problem.

'At least we know the tension is real. But it feels like it's going to burst right out,' I said to John after Nick had gone to hit the waves.

It didn't take long for that to happen.

Late one night, Nalinda turned up again unannounced, his evening intrusions had been becoming more frequent. He ordered a drink, sat on a sofa next to some guests who were having a nightcap and told them he was the owner and that he and his wife had done an excellent job managing the hotel.

Vinod came to our room to tell me, 'Mrs Dasha, maybe one problem with Nalinda. Here.'

I watched with John through the venetian blinds of our front room window onto the courtyard, which acted as a one-way mirror. We could see out, but no one could see in. What we saw was a problem that was getting worse. And it wasn't going away.

Nick had discussed Nalinda's drinking problem as a thing of the past. But maybe it wasn't the case.

'But where are the managers? What are they doing? They should be here. Why aren't they here?' Nalinda loudly demanded of the few guests still up late. They all looked away and left to go to their rooms one by one.

The next day, after Nick had returned to London, John emailed him a progress report, saying we had reached a tipping point. Nalinda's ill-defined role had led to increasingly unpredictable and angry behaviour. He'd come unannounced for the second night that week, behaving inappropriately towards the guests.

John also listed the daily practical problems we faced – the circuit breakers were still tripping out, cutting power to the restaurant, kitchen bar and garden lighting, with the main over-rider even catching fire.

His fury was palpable through the screen:

We spend vast amounts of time putting out fires (metaphorically speaking, usually) due to systems' failure. We do this in an environment where your local partner continually undermines us, has informed you he hates us and wants to sack all the staff because they don't respect him.

We didn't hear back and three days later, John and I left to go to Colombo for the weekend to escape the tension, nervous about what we would find on our return.

Chapter 20

SUNSET SHOWDOWN

'Stay where you are. Don't go back to the hotel. Nalinda says he wants to kill John. Wait there in Colombo till he calms down.'

That's where we were when Nick's brittle phone call left us feeling jangled and threatened.

Nalinda had searched the office computer after we left for Colombo, found John's progress report on the desktop, read it and deleted it. Deeply insulted because of John's criticisms of his inappropriate behaviour toward some guests, he had phoned Nick announcing that he wanted to kill John.

He rejected everything that John had written. 'It's all lies,' Nalinda said. And now his fury was lashing us in Colombo, all the way from Hikkaduwa.

We bolted from the Perahera cavalcade of sequined elephants back to our Colombo four-star refuge. Our dream of paradise was fast morphing into hell.

'Looks like we've lobbed a live grenade.' But we both agreed at the time it was a careful explanation of an impossible situation.

'Just too bad you left the report on the desktop and didn't file it away. Out of sight. Did you do that on purpose, John?' No answer.

John was unusually quiet. His bulk sat stock still as he slowly smoked a cigarette, his face impassive like carved marble. Unreadable.

A dizzying clash of thoughts collided in my mind while I paced around our suite. With its lounge area, dining table and swish bathroom, it had seemed heaven-sent when we were upgraded on check-in; now it felt like a cage.

'What are we going to do? Do you really think Nalinda wants to kill you because of what he read in the report? Can we make this right? Is it too late?'

Sphinx-like, he replied, 'I don't know. But I guess we'll have to go back and find out.'

'It might seem logical to you, but I don't feel too good about it. I mean, who's going to have our back? Nick? He's made it clear he's not on our side. Maybe we should stay in Colombo for a while? It'd be safer.' John was hunting through the mini-bar, looking for solace.

I reminded John of the story we'd heard about a manager at a hotel in the Galle Fort. That after she'd fired the security guard he said he'd kill her. The hotel had to hire an escort guard to accompany her home every day. In the end she left Sri Lanka.'

The miniature bottles of gin, vodka and whisky we drank from the mini-bar didn't illuminate anything for us; *in vino veritas* failed. We slumped into a fitful sleep.

The genie was out of the bottle, and we had no idea how to stuff it back in.

The following morning, I realised that John was right; we did have to go back. It was the only way to know if Nalinda's threat was real. Or not.

I picked away at my nail polish, lying in the oversized bed that could fit a family of four. The kind of bed with a brocaded forest of pillows you have to fight through to get into the bed. I called out to John, trying to convince myself.

'Helen and Victoria are arriving this afternoon. We've gotta be there to greet them. Besides, we can't hide out in Colombo wondering if Nalinda's threat is real, can we?'

John was shaving in the bathroom in a large fluffy white towel, wrapped sarong style.

He stepped into the doorway and waved his razor in the air like the conductor of an imaginary orchestra. 'Well, going back is the only way to find out if he's just piss and wind'.'

John's devil-may-care attitude scared me, and my heart was beating faster than it should. No one had ever threatened my life before, or anyone close to me. There was no guide map I could google on what to do. Our fragile new world as hotel managers was sliding down a slippery slope on a tuk-tuk out of control.

And anyway, what do you do in a situation like this?

I couldn't think of a single movie to help me out. No one's life got threatened in *The Best Exotic Marigold Hotel*. And it wasn't something that Lonely Planet guides provided recommendations on.

We left Colombo later that morning, shell-shocked as we travelled back to the hotel we had poured our hearts and souls into for the last eight months. We sat wordlessly the whole way, locked in our own thoughts, gazing out the car's windows at the familiar, maniacal, fluid traffic chaos on Galle Road. Cars pressed bumper to bumper, moving only inches at a time, horns continually beeping, tuk-tuks darting like mosquitoes on suicide missions, in improvised four lanes of traffic on a road made for two. One tuk-tuk passed perilously close to us, its rear roof canopy emblazoned with the slogan:

CHE GUEVARA WANTS YOU TO REBEL

It seemed appropriate.

Whether it was an accidental or an intentional oversight on John's part to leave the report on the desktop, I will never ever know.

Born in the Chinese Year of the Monkey, John was prone to be mischievous, impulsive and deliberately provocative when bored. He could proudly sport a 'fuck-you' attitude if he felt the situation called for it. Not that everyone always shared his sentiment or sense of humour.

He incurred the wrath of the blue-blazered, gold-buttoned LA-based Paramount Studio Heads while he was the creative consultant at Foxtel's Comedy Channel. He designed a PR key-ring tag to send to the press. One side read: 'If found, return to the Comedy Channel.' On the flip side, 'We'll pinch the car and go you halves'. When presented with a sample the blazer brigade was not amused. They didn't want to sell their shows to a channel with such questionable morals; but the key-ring was a hit with the press in Australia.

But it was no time for jokes now.

Our mistake was underestimating how rigid and hierarchical the social system was. Sri Lankans are so conscious of the social order and their status in it that it pervades every aspect of their lives.

In hindsight, we understood that we'd attacked Nalinda in the most fundamental way. We now know that losing face in Asian cultures is *the* big issue. Not that safeguarding one's reputation is less important in other cultures, but causing someone to lose face in Asia can cause you to lose yours. Hindsight, as Billy Wilder once said, is always 20-20.

We had thrown down the gauntlet even if we hadn't realised it, and there would be repercussions.

Again Nick's words from when we first arrived in Hikkaduwa rang in my ears: 'When voices are raised, machetes come out.'

Another tuk-tuk scudded by, within inches of the car window.

Lost in our thoughts, I realised, too late, that we'd missed the freeway turn-off.

Without telling us, the driver had decided he didn't want to pay the $US5 toll. We were now locked into a three-hour-long journey back on a crowded one-lane road heading south – a road shared with buses, cars, motorcycles, bicycles, bullock drays and the occasional cow.

The coastal sand strip that was slammed up against the railway line right next to our potholed road was fringed with wild fecundity. Breadfruit trees, traveller's palms, cashew trees, betel nut and banana palms, threaded with temple flower trees, all jostled each other for space amongst poorly maintained village buildings.

Not only would it be a slow ride back, it was uncomfortable; with no air conditioning and a driver who didn't seem to notice his radio was off-station most of the time. Discomfort magnified.

The last half of the trip was also visually shocking, a grim reminder of the impact of the tsunami that had decimated the island eight years earlier. We passed through village after abandoned village that had become cemeteries, with the debris of smashed-up buildings still mouldering away.

Texts were criss-crossing the globe between Nick in London and us in Hikkaduwa. We needed Nalinda to leave the office keys with Vinod so we could access the hotel safe where we kept our passports and our money. Nick said he would speak to Nalinda.

It was mid-afternoon when we crunched onto the familiar gravel driveway of our modest colonial-bungalow-fronted hotel. Out in the courtyard, Vinod, Suresh and Jayantha greeted us warmly, but no one had the office keys and they'd not heard from Nalinda.

Reggae beats murmured away from the bar sound system; the sun gently basted the hotel guests slumbering on the sun lounges; the rolling surf lapped the shoreline. The thick frangipani-scented air was signalling siesta time. Everything was deceptively tranquil.

Our Aussie friends Helen and Victoria arrived late in the afternoon, settling into their rooms in our 'tropical paradise' before having cocktails in the courtyard, and watching yet another magnificent sunset. The sky blazed into the saturated hallucinogenic colour of a Turner landscape on steroids, that familiar brilliant orange, rich red and bright purple streaking as far as our eyes could swivel.

It was an extravaganza Hikkaduwa was famous for. And something we could always promise our guests – brilliant sunsets accompanied by ice-cold drinks.

Around 15 people were chilling out in the front courtyard facing the sunset, drinking Mojitos and Surfside Specials, listening to the cool jazz guitar playlist that DJ Helen had brought us.

Two hours had gone by since our return. John texted Nalinda continually, asking for our keys to be returned.

No response.

'Just stay cool,' we told each other.

As the light subsided into that liminal moment between day and night, I was mingling, lighting candles for the guests on the small courtyard tables. In my peripheral vision I caught sight of Nalinda. He stood some 15 metres away, on the boundary of the hotel's courtyard and the beachfront, his bronzed face contorted with rage, his eyes bulging and blazing like one of the devil masks in the Ambalangoda mask museum.

I looked for John. He was behind me, on full alert, in the hotel doorway. Nalinda was walking towards us, yelling in English.

'Get out, you bloody bastard, get out, get out now.'

Nalinda's words turned into a torrent in Sinhala, leading one guest witnessing this to tell me later that she thought he was a random menacing madman who'd come off the beach threatening the guests in the hotel.

My throat clamped tight, fear rising all the way from my clenched pelvic floor. Vinod shrank into the shadows behind the bar, trying to be invisible.

Suddenly, I could see exactly what was about to happen, like those few seconds before impact in a car crash.

I looked at Nalinda's fists, clenched in rage. He was about to throw a punch at John.

Towering over him and never shy of a physical fight, I knew that John would slug him back.

The police would come.

Foreigners against a local.

A local who was a friend of the police. The odds were stacked against us.

We'd be done for.

Grabbing John by the arm, I pulled him backwards, 'You've got to go into our room. Right now. Go. Go.'

Before he could respond, I pushed him back down the hotel corridor. Then, opening our door with one hand, I tried pushing him into our room, but he pushed back.

'No, no, I'm staying with you.'

But this wasn't the time for John's male pride to confront Nalinda head-on.

'If you stay you'll make it worse. That's what he wants. To take you on. Pleeeease don't do it. Call Nick. Tell him what's happening right now.'

I grabbed the door handle, pushed him back into the room and pulled the door shut.

'Call Nick,' I yelled through the door. 'Text him. Tell him what's happening; tell him he has to do something! He has to call Nalinda.'

I turned. Nalinda was advancing towards me like a cobra.

I faced Nalinda head-on, drawing up my full 1.6-metre height. He was now dead square in front of me, his fists clenched.

I took a deep breath.

'So…' I asked in a quiet voice, staring straight into his furious eyes, 'Do you hit women?'

The words fell out of my mouth, I had no idea where they came from. Why did I choose those words? A mystery at the time, and still is. There had been gossip amongst the staff that Nalinda would hit his wife when he got drunk. But no one had seen evidence of this.

My *sotto voce* challenge stopped him dead in his tracks. His eyes still ablaze, 'No, I never hit woman.'

His clenched fists uncurled. I knew the moment of danger had passed.

'Good. Then give me the keys to the office. Immediately. You are illegally withholding our passports in the safe.'

'Go to the police then,' he sneered.

I was standing close enough to smell alcohol. Maybe the immediate danger was gone, but I could tell he would still be difficult.

'Give me the keys. Now. Right now. And stop making a problem in front of the guests. We'll talk about this in the office. Not here.'

By now, the guests in the courtyard had turned to watch this sunset showdown with quizzical looks on their faces.

Not a good look for a 'tranquil hotel paradise'.

Without another word, I signalled Nalinda to follow me down the long corridor to the office. When we got to the door, he refused to unlock it, relishing his control of the moment.

I kept at him. 'You have no right to do this. We need our passports and our money immediately. Please give me the keys now!'

Nalinda started yelling, 'I don't trust you. I won't give you keys. Go to the police then, tell them!'

Long minutes went by.

John kept calling Nick in London.

Nick kept calling Nalinda to calm him down and to persuade him to hand over the keys.

After a long bluster, Nalinda finally agreed to hand me the keys. But on one proviso.

I had to wait while he went out into the courtyard and returned with one of the guests reluctantly trailing down the corridor. Finally, the keys were handed over to me; I opened the safe, and Nalinda made the embarrassed guest inspect the contents and witness how much money was there.

I took our passports and our money for safekeeping in our room.

Nalinda stormed out of the hotel into the night with his sad-eyed wife, who had appeared from nowhere. He took a small black metal box with all the remaining petty cash.

I went back to our room to tell John it was over. As I opened the door, he abruptly ended his call to Nick and rushed over to me.

We hugged each other very tightly, as I stilled my body's sudden involuntary shaking, wrapped up in John's big bearhug embrace.

Although Nalinda had roared off on his scooter with his wife perched on its back, he wasn't quite done for the night.

Vinod was relishing the drama as he came to tell me.

'Mrs Dasha, Nalinda, he phones, he tells me, John and Dasha are very dangerous, stealing money. You have to watch them. They can't be trusted. Don't give them any food and drinks.'

War was officially declared.

There was no coming back from such a bitter confrontation. Nalinda had knowingly crossed the line.

And so had we. We had caused Nalinda to 'lose face' even more in front of his business partner. Stripped of respect, he would stop at nothing to get rid of us now.

Some days later, when I told a nearby café owner our story of the Sunset Showdown, he nodded knowingly.

'If you threaten a Sri Lankan man's status and privileges, they go crazy.'

Over the next few days, there was a furious exchange of emails between Nick and us – back and forth, forth and back. We were looking for protection while he tried to assure us there was no danger: 'Can you just put the Sunset Showdown behind you and find a way to work with Nalinda?'

One email in this exchange confirmed our suspicion that Nalinda and his wife were never told the truth about why we were brought in to replace them as managers. Nick wrote to us that he hadn't, 'for obvious reasons', made it clear to Nalinda why he was bringing in two people to run the hotel. He claimed that he didn't explain, again for 'obvious reasons', that Nalinda couldn't do the job to the level he wanted. Nor, he went on to say, had he made it clear to Nalinda that he needed him to help and cooperate with us at all times.

We never did find out what the 'obvious reasons' were. But it was too late to wonder by that stage in the saga.

At breakfast, the coconut sambal didn't taste like paradise anymore.

John pushed his scrambled eggs around the plate.

I was worried. We didn't seem to have any options left. We were vulnerable to Nalinda, with no real support from Nick, and no recourse with the police.

'What happens if he blows up and threatens us again? Do we call the High Commission in Colombo? What could they do? Nothing! We're really on our own here. I'm so angry.'

'Okay, Dasha, I get it.' John snapped.

'We're under siege. I don't want to leave this place any more than you do. But no one's got our back, we're not safe. And I'm fed up.'

John stood up and walked away.

I sent an email to Nick outlining my loss of confidence in him because he'd failed to provide a strategy to protect us.

In reply, Nick assured us there was nothing to be concerned about; we just had to wait for Nalinda to calm down and for things to blow over. We didn't feel safe or reassured.

Early in the morning, three nail-biting days later, John and I were huddled together over a fine brew of Sri Lankan breakfast tea as I twisted a paper napkin through my fingers. An eerie truce had descended between Nalinda and us.

Meaning no further incidents had occurred. But we felt like sitting ducks, abandoned and hung out to dry. We started to think we didn't have a choice; we had to leave. And we had to tell Nick.

John watched as two hotel housekeepers underwent the early morning ritual of hoisting the sun umbrellas on the beachfront. He turned in his chair to face me.

'Maybe it's best not to put an exact date on it. But to say it's imminent. Because if we announce when we're going, God knows what stunt Nalinda might pull.'

After two more sleepless nights of feverish discussion, going round and round in circles, we were convinced there remained nothing more we could do.

Except leave.

Chapter 21

EXIT STAGE LEFT

Saturday arrived, and both of us were up early after another sleepless night. We were going about the usual hotel routine, watching the breakfast service while trying to appear nonchalant. But we both confessed to each other that our stomachs were somersaulting.

John smoked several throat-tearing local-brand Hollywood cigarettes in quick succession. I mournfully downed a cup of tea but, unusually, couldn't face food. Apart from saying how dreadful we felt, we didn't talk. Today was the day we'd decided we were leaving. Silently and swiftly.

Our bags were packed and stashed in the hotel's front office at the roadside gate. When I scanned the tables of guests having breakfast, I spotted our friend Andrew, a senior official at the Australian High Commission, with his wife and children. They'd appeared unannounced, having come to Hikkaduwa for a Saturday surf break from Colombo.

It was perfect timing. We needed his advice and someone official to know what was going on. John agreed. I grabbed the large Vegemite jar we kept just for Australians. No other nationality appreciated this salty, spreadable, black tar on toast first thing in the morning.

'Good to see you all here,' I said breezily, placing the Vegemite in the centre of the table. 'I thought you might like a taste of home with your toast.'

Andrew introduced me to his wife, Katrina, and their two young children. We made small talk about the surf conditions.

'Andrew, could you spare me a minute when you finish breakfast? There's something I'd like your advice on.' I mustn't have sounded as cool as I thought; I saw a cloud pass over his face.

'Sure. I'll come over when we're finished.'

Twenty minutes later, he joined us. 'What's up?'

'Hmmm... John and I have a difficult situation here,' I blurted out.

John said nothing. But a slight nod of his head encouraged me to continue, and the story tumbled out.

'Have you come across threats like this before?' John asked. 'Dasha's worried...'

'In fact,' I jumped in, 'we're planning to leave today. Do you think we're overreacting?'

Andrew considered his words carefully.

'Well, I can't say exactly without knowing all the details. But judging by what we've seen at the Commission when Australians are involved in business with Sri Lankan partners and it goes bad, I would say it could be serious. Terrible things happen here that never get reported in the media or by the police.'

Andrew proceeded to tell us the story of one Australian businessman whose import and export business with a Sri Lankan partner went belly up. The partner burnt down the warehouse, leaving the Australian with nothing.

He then went on to describe how, along our beach, there were two British girls raped, allegedly by police. Not long ago. Not reported to anyone.

'Would you advise us to leave?' I squeaked out in a rising voice.

'If you can do that easily and quickly, then yes, I would say that would be your best option.'

An intense panic was rising, flooding my mind. I took a deep breath and exhaled slowly – it's supposed to work in yoga classes, but it didn't have much effect.

John had his hands clasped on top of the table, his eyes cast down at them, not betraying anything.

'Now I feel anxious,' I said.

'Let me go and get Katrina. She's better to talk to about this stuff; she works on the assistance of Australian citizens side of things.'

'Well, that nails it, Dasha. We're out of here.'

Katrina's calm, matter-of-fact manner suggested we weren't the first Australians to be in trouble in Sri Lanka.

'If anything should go wrong, call this number. It's my mobile, and I can put you onto someone if you need help.'

'Thanks very much.' My panic subsided. I didn't feel we were quite so alone.

We shook hands, and Andrew and Katrina left with the family to hit the beach.

John and I sat looking at each other. I tried to sound confident, 'Well, we have a number to call. Let's hope we don't need it.'

John stood up.

'Let's get going.'

'Are you worried?'

'Nup,' dropping his voice so no one could eavesdrop.

'We have to get out of here before Nalinda shows up. I'll organise a car.'

Everything was ready to go.

A car and driver waited outside the hotel with all our bags on board; our final email to Nick, written early that morning, was ready to go on hitting *Send*.

John got Jayantha to come to the office so we could tell him that we were leaving, right now.

Jayantha's large sad eyes widened in shock.

'Please know that you and all the staff have been so fantastic, and we'll miss working with you very much.' John pulled a wad of notes from his pocket.

'Here's some money that I want you to share with the others. It's 5000 rupees each to thank you all for your hard work in helping us get the hotel up and running. Please say goodbye to Suresh, Latith and Vinod, and tell them how very sorry we are that we can't speak to them.' John handed him the cash.

The three of us stood mutely, looking at each other, emotionally overwhelmed. We all teared up, moving in to share a big embrace.

Tears streamed down my face as we pulled away. John continued, 'I'll text Nalinda right now, explaining that we've left and given you the keys to the office, and he can collect them from you. Okay, Jayantha?'

We hugged one another again, trying to hold onto the moment before I broke away to walk outside to the car.

I stood outside the front door in the driveway and looked back into the hotel at the two welcome bowls on either side of the door filled with floating frangipanis and the woven cane lampshade hanging in the lobby that John had designed. My eyes travelled down through the long gallery-style corridor, lined with Dominic Sansoni's beautiful photos, towards the courtyard with the sea beyond, and my tears kept falling as I bit my lip to stifle a sob. This wasn't the way for our dream of paradise to end, or for us to leave the place we had poured our hearts into.

John went into the hotel office to press *Send* on our last email as managers of the hotel to Nick.

> *There is a very clear threat to our safety in remaining here. We warned you that Nalinda was at explosion point. He has continued to appear unannounced and at inappropriate times despite the terms you claimed to have negotiated with him.*
>
> *You made clear promises to us that Nalinda would know what our brief was, but now we understand that the working relationship was never explained to him or his family properly from the beginning.*
>
> *We see these issues as fundamental to our forced departure. This email is written with great sadness on our part.*
>
> *We believe we have exceeded expectations and are leaving you with a hotel successfully re-imaged and re-positioned in the market. In just twenty weeks we took the place from an unsanitary mess below the radar to the number three beach-strip hotel on Trip Adviser, while having to spend half our time patching over huge cracks to keep it functioning and wrangling an increasingly recalcitrant Nalinda.*
>
> *Two Australian Commission staff members are present at Surfside today and are aware of our situation.*
>
> *John Pinder and Dasha Ross*

While I sat in the back of the hire car with all our bags, John fired off texts to Nalinda in Hikkaduwa and Nick in London, telling them we had left the hotel and entrusted the office keys to Jayantha.

It was over. I couldn't believe it.

John enveloped me in his arms as we drove out the hotel gates for the last time. Clinging to each other, we were lost in sad silence.

It hadn't worked out. If only, if only, if only... But what?

We would have never been able to overcome Nalinda's determination to get rid of us. John's phone pinged in his pocket with a text from Nalinda saying, 'What you mean leaving?'

I looked out the window at the familiar road as we drove past the jewellers, the woodcarvers, the shops selling sarongs and tourist paintings, the cafés with names like The Munchy Shack, and the Starbeans café with its replica Starbucks' logo. Village dogs roamed in a desultory fashion along the roadside, trying to work out when it was safe to make a dash for the other side. Many didn't make it. We were both pissed off that Nalinda had screwed up our plans to run the hotel. Angry that Nick didn't tell us the truth from the beginning. Or tell Nalinda. And really annoyed that Nalinda won. And Nick had let him. But if truth be told, there was also a sense of relief. That we wouldn't have to keep fighting a losing battle.

John looked sideways out the window at the streetscape we knew so well by now. The roadside Buddha encased in a mounted glass shrine, crowned by a halo of flashing rainbow lights, seemed to be winking at us.

We lapsed into silence, watching the familiar lush green scenery, narrow coastal strip and more roadside disco Buddhas whoosh by.

'It'll make a funny story one day,' John squeezed my hand and pulled me close. We shared a long, lingering kiss. We had each other, forever locked together, more strongly than before – co-pilots on a plane to adventure to places unknown.

I couldn't help but smile, 'And don't forget the book we're going to write. We could call it *Eat, Pray, Run.*'

That made him laugh.

A few days later, we hovered in suspended animation in a five-star Colombo hotel, waiting for a late-night flight back to Sydney. Drained and weighed down by anxiety that would only lift when we cleared customs.

The cocktail pianist concentrated hard on the baby grand in the hotel foyer. She was playing 'The Last Waltz'. It seemed like a fitting farewell.

Chapter 22

I'VE DONE IT ALL

Fireworks explode in vast spheres above our heads, showering us in hot gold, shimmering silver and shocking pink stars, illuminating a black velvet winter sky over the waves of Bondi Beach.

The fireworks canisters carry John's ashes as far as they can into the universe. Below us, on the apron of the Bondi Beach Icebergs ocean pool, a giant plywood cut-out of John's signature yellow glasses ignites, studded with 150 yellow cigarette-sized tubes of a pyrotechnic compound.

Over 200 people cram the balconies of the Bondi Icebergs Club overlooking the pool, crying, clapping and cheering. Our daughter Lola and I cling to each other, sobbing and gulping air, as we strain to look outwards to sea, through the cascade of fireworks.

Our ringmaster has left the tent.

The words of his beloved American satirist George Carlin, are hanging in the air: 'Give them a show when you go, do something to capture their imagination.'

John gave one directive before he died: we were not to hold a funeral service. Instead, we must host a big party with an endless open bar, funny stories to be told, ending with the grand finale of his ashes being blasted into space in a trajectory of fireworks sparks over the Bondi sea.

He wanted it to be a spectacle celebrating his legacy, so he spent the last six weeks of his life producing it to ensure it was; organising who would MC the event, put on the fireworks display, and tell funny stories about him. He was in control of his last show until his last breath.

His long-time friend and colleague Wendy Harmer wrote John's obituary in *The Australian* newspaper:

> *As a kid, the comedy impresario lived next to a circus lot in Oamaru, NZ, and he never lost his wide-eyed wonder and delight in all things improbable and daring. In John Pinder's universe, to fly was to launch into the blue yonder beyond the heights one thought possible. To fail was to land with a mere earthly bump. Like the circus trouper he was, Pinder dusted off the sawdust and tried again, each time higher, faster, further.*

'Further' was one of John's mantras. It was inspired by Tom Wolfe's book *The Electric Kool-Aid Acid Test*, which recounted how Ken Kesey and his merry pranksters drove a psychedelic bus, fuelled by acid and mayhem, from California to New York in 1964. The manifest on the 1939 International Harvester school bus read FURTHUR. That's where John always believed you should and could go.

And on his explicit instructions, that's where we sent him.

* * *

Some weeks after John and I had returned to Sydney from Sri Lanka, a routine medical check-up led to a shocking discovery. John had Stage 4 muscle-invasive bladder cancer, despite having no noticeable symptoms. But he had been a dedicated smoker for most of his adult life, and research revealed that smoking was a known cause in half of all bladder cancers in both men and women. Nine months of soul-destroying treatment ensued. A radical cystectomy operation removing his bladder and prostate gland, followed by five months of gut-wrenching (literally) chemotherapy and radiation therapy.

I navigated John through the complex and often contradictory cancer-care maze, as he was too shell-shocked, opioid affected and ill to want to know anything about his illness. At all.

I compensated for his disconnection by voraciously ingesting everything I could on his form of cancer. From national and international online bladder cancer forums to force-reading *The Emperor of all Maladies* – an all-encompassing complex and mammoth-sized biography of cancer by an oncologist and assistant professor of medicine at Columbia University, Dr Siddhartha Mukherjee.

I thought that this knowledge would arm me, help me to help John turn the tide against his insidious disease. I couldn't and wouldn't accept that he would or could die. I was convinced, above all else, that he would recover.

The horror of what was happening to him, to us, kept escalating, with my take-out memories of this treatment period reduced to two things: one, that the urologist never used the 'C' word when talking to us; coyly referring only to the 'tumour'; and two, that John's eight-hour surgery to remove his bladder and prostate gland had to fit in with the surgeon's schedule to go to Lords, in London, to watch the Test Cricket.

Sri Lanka receded, shimmering only as a palm-fringed mirage in our memories. We'd fallen out of paradise and entered into cancer's hell.

During this sad, bad time, there was one concept I clung to.

Despite the crazy times, the myriad of frustrations and the chaotic dramas we endured running the place we called Faulty

Palms, it shone as the very best of times in all our years of marriage.

In Sri Lanka, we became a couple in the truest sense. An equal partnership, totally in sync and working as an interlocked team to realise a shared dream. We were creating new possibilities for our future together that we had never considered before, nor even thought remotely possible.

But there were many times, deep in the night, during John's months of illness, that I was gripped and paralysed by the darkest of my fears about losing him, and this sustaining concept of our coupledom would fade from my mind's eye.

Six months after all his post-operative treatments concluded, John was told his cancer was in remission and that it would be safe for us to leave Australia and return to Spain to live.

We had lived in Barcelona for some months just before we headed to Sri Lanka and had fallen crazily in love with this city.

We fully embraced its inclusive, open, aesthetically conscious and vibrant lifestyle, the socially just awareness of our friends there, and the democratic local politics: the fact that foreigners like us were fluidly welcomed and enveloped into the communal life on offer.

We had decided to apply for Spanish residency and return to live in Barcelona after finishing the tourist season in Sri Lanka. Now John was even more determined to re-embrace this original plan.

We applied for and got Spanish residency, allowing us to take off on one more adventure, to live out one more dream. We wanted to harness all we had learnt running Faulty Palms and apply it in Barcelona by buying and managing a tourist-licensed short-stay apartment. This would provide us with income while we explored creative opportunities. I would write freelance articles, and John would be the Executive Producer of productions for the Edinburgh Festival.

Emboldened that John's cancer was in remission, we sold our place in Bondi, put half of our belongings in storage, and shipped the other half in boxes to Barcelona. We would begin a new life together on the other side of the world.

Landing in Barcelona, we found a captivating Art Nouveau style apartment, through luck and connections, to rent in the Eixample barrio. The apartment building was constructed at the turn of the 20th century and had enormous charm and lofty space, with six-metre-high wooden front doors, an Art Nouveau painted ceiling setting off the lobby chandelier, and a wood-panelled caged elevator that was straight out of a Hitchcock movie.

We bought up big at IKEA and started to put down roots.

And while we did land and did settle, our dream never got total lift-off.

* * *

Eight months later, I packed our lives back into the boxes that brought our possessions to Spain, and we returned to Australia. A routine check-up scan had revealed that John's cancer had returned with a vengeance. Terminal. Metastasising throughout his pelvic bones, spine and thigh bones.

Back in Bondi, from late spring through to the onset of winter, I found John's final physical disintegration harrowing. An unspeakable experience I could only witness helplessly. There was nothing I could do to prevent it.

I pushed my feelings down, deep, deep down, refusing to accept it was happening. I was incapable of believing it. I always had faith that he could and would turn it around. Like before.

One day passed into another. Balancing John's medical care, fighting off my mounting despair at even the possibility of losing him and our life together, while living daily with a phalanx of doctors telling me he would die. I still wouldn't, couldn't believe that there were no miracles on offer.

We forgot about paradise.

John spent the last months of his life very peacefully, in the tender care of nurses and much morphine in the small palliative wing of a large Sydney hospital. He had stoically accepted what he saw as the final roll of his dice with great grace. He refused the metaphor of 'fighting' cancer.

'There is no contest. It's a ravaging disease that will kill me, and I can decide how to accept that,' he said with a pragmatic stillness.

John had no belief in any existence beyond this one and, not having faith of any persuasion, believed that everything came to a screeching halt with his last breath. He told everybody that he had lived his life exactly as he wanted and had done everything he'd ever desired. He pronounced loudly that nothing was left undone and that he had no regrets about anything.

He roared at a nurse who dared to ask him one day if anything was left on his bucket list, 'I don't have a fucking bucket list; I've done it all.'

During his last three months, I sat with him every day in his small sun-dappled ward, passing the time together, reading the newspapers with him, and talking randomly about people and events in our lives. That is, when the morphine subsided sufficiently to leave him some clarity.

One day I asked him if he had been terror-stricken when Nalinda threatened to kill him.

'Nah, I was bored. We'd done what we went to do,' he said, his bright eyes wide open.

For a fleeting moment, I saw John as he'd always been – ebullient, mischievous and emphatic.

'We were paid shit money; Nalinda would never give up until we were gone. We'd completed the most interesting part of rebranding and relaunching the hotel. After that, it was boring hard work serving the customers, and I'd had enough.'

I was stunned.

'Are you for real? Don't you remember how Nick told us that when voices are raised in Sri Lanka, the machetes come out?'

John shrugged his wasted, bony shoulders; his eyes closed as he sank back into the hospital bed.

I will never know whether it was his morphine bravado speaking or, in the face of an inescapable death threat, the past couldn't compete and didn't matter anymore.

* * *

I was shattered and traumatised when John died.

Beyond any words I could name to explain the pain.

An inexplicable rage howled inside me, wanting to scream, scream until I had no breath left. But this rage was against what exactly?

While he stoically accepted his fate, John didn't choose to die. He was just 70 years old with so much living still to do.

So how could I be angry with him? For abandoning me to this black-as-black inward-looking, vortex of self-pity? For leaving the tent when we were only just over halfway through our performance together?

I had no answers – only the horror of suffocating sadness. I'd lost my soul mate, our life together, and our dreams. My dreams. What kind of life was left without him?

I couldn't face up to that unbearable question.

I searched many books to find some roadmap for grief to help guide me. But none of them stilled the searing pain inside me as I shuddered and sobbed for weeks and weeks and weeks.

I stopped listening to music except for just one song that I played repeatedly. Day after day. Over, over, over, and again at a deafening volume through headphones so I could feel it blasting through my body. 'Don't Leave Me This Way', by

Harold Melvin & The Blue Notes. Screaming out the lyrics was the only way I could give voice to my agony: 'I can't exist, I will surely miss, Your tender kiss...'

Well-meaning friends tried to comfort me by telling me how lucky I was to have had the time to say goodbye, having been told that John's illness was terminal six months earlier. But nothing, nothing, prepared me for his death when it came and, with it, my headlong plunge into a soulless black hole.

The only comfort I clung onto was that John's death was very gentle and peaceful.

I was in his hospice room, lying awake beside him at 2 am, when I heard his breathing change. His in-breaths became shallow, accelerating sharply.

Then his breathing stopped. Just stopped.

I jumped up and grabbed hold of him as an image flooded my mind, of John running along a very high diving board and then plunging off its end into space.

Buddhist lamas say that when our mind departs our body, death occurs, and we enter the bardo state. I watched that moment when John's essence left his body. All I was left with was a cold carapace. The shell that he'd inhabited for 70 years. And I knew then the intolerable truth – I would never see him again. Perhaps in my dreams, but not as a hovering spirit.

I saw. I felt. I knew at that moment sitting with him. Dead is dead.

Gone forever.

***

In the following months, only one book came close to etching the sorrow in my grief-struck world. Julian Barnes wrote about the death of his wife in his essay, 'The Loss of Depth', from his book *Levels of Life*:

... And as E.M. Forster put it, "One death may explain itself, but it throws no light upon another." So grief in turn becomes unimaginable: not just its length and depth, but its tone and texture, its deceptions and false dawns, its recidivism. Also, its initial shock: you have suddenly come down in the freezing German Ocean, equipped only with an absurd cork jacket that is supposed to keep you alive. And you can never prepare for this new reality in which you have been dunked.

Barnes' raw and sparse prose perfectly echoed my madness, loneliness and despair. And there was just one object from our life together that brought me any solace, a giant, beribboned, grey flannel cushion that I had bought in Colombo, emblazoned with large embroidered neon pink letters:

Maybe some women aren't meant to be tamed.
 Maybe they need to run free
Until they find someone just as wild
To run with them!

John was my someone, my ringmaster, my rock tethering my kite as I flew high and higher in my career; he orchestrated an exciting, chaotic, sometimes maddening, curiosity-driven life that we shared with our daughter.

Looking at the cushion, propped on my bed, many months after John died, I was gripped with a driving propulsion.

'I have to go back to Sri Lanka.'

Chapter 23

HIS SPIRIT LIVES ON

Three years after we fled and one year after John died, I stopped off in Sri Lanka on my way back to Australia from a family reunion in Europe.

An inexplicable magnetic force had pulled me back to where we had been so happy together.

I arrived to feel the comfort of being enveloped by the soggy blanket of humid heat. Seeing all the white goods still being sold duty-free at Colombo airport and all the men and women wearing clothes in the saturated colours of that oh-so-familiar Sri Lankan sunset.

Everything felt familiar and nostalgic. Slowly I noticed subtle signs of change, highlighting the growing influx of tourists. Giant banners at the airport proclaimed that malaria had been eradicated. The Galle Face Hotel was recovering from a radical facelift, losing its shabby chic patina to become a solid five-star glossy hotel. The Duke of Edinburgh's car was still on proud public display but in the hotel's new marble-floored museum. No longer in the foyer.

Squads of Chinese tourists replaced the previously seen Russian packs prowling around the tiny cobbled streets of the Galle Fort. On the coastal road between Colombo and Galle, a newly completed 500-room Chinese-owned hotel for Chinese tourists had just opened. They were the latest influx for Sri Lankans to complain about.

'They have no manners,' said one hotel owner.

'They have no respect for buying,' a gemstone merchant told me.

These were the same complaints I used to hear Sri Lankans make about Russian tourists.

'They give with one hand and take with the other,' claimed a café owner, talking about the new highway between Colombo and Galle. Built with Chinese investment, the collected tolls are repaid to Chinese investors.

I installed myself in a hotel back in Hikkaduwa, just a 10-minute walk up the manic Galle Road from 'our' Surfside Hotel. Curiosity pulled me towards it on the first day I was in the village, when I peered cautiously over the metre-high front wall. The sizeable illuminated street sign John designed was still next to the entrance with his proud tagline under the hotel's name.

John's spirit lives on here.

But an invisible force barred me from going through the open gateway. An unnamed apprehension.

I turned around and went back to my hotel.

The village's main road remained unchanged except for three new speed bumps installed to slow down the suicide-mission buses. The bumps added a new thrill-seeking dimension as the buses abseiled over the top, not attempting to slow down.

Déjà vu continued with the sarong and clothes shops selling the same stock from when we were there; the woodcarvers still hawking the same bug-eyed devil masks, elephants of all sizes, and statues of fishermen on poles; snack places with names like 'The Cool Spot' still served the same food. The lace maker was still hand-making the same intricate piece in the front of her shop.

It took me three days to summon up the courage to break through the emotional force field. On the third day, I set off with my head down, my eyes fixed on the road, trying hard to compose my emotions, as I was unsure who or what I might encounter if I made it through the front gate.

I stand in 'our' hotel's gateway and push myself through the invisible barrier by turning in past the recently painted front fence. Walking with reluctant, heavy feet through the open front door, everything looks familiar yet changed. The first thing I notice is that our art-directed lobby has gone. The TV has been moved back to the roadside front of the hotel for the staff to watch. Once again, hotel arrivals are greeted by staff sitting around on broken furniture, watching a blaring TV. And there are no welcome bowls with flowers on either side of the entrance.

I walk down the long dark corridor with its 12 rooms, six on either side, and step out onto the courtyard. My heart is beating faster and faster, my breathing shallower with each step, and my dread rising, settling as a weight on my chest.

My eyes prickle with tears that I blink away, and an overwhelming sob starts in my throat that I keep swallowing to suppress.

Is it because I am stepping back in time? Is it the grief of losing John?

Do I fear encountering Nalinda? I know that he is back running the hotel. Just as he always had.

I have no explanation – just a thumping in my chest.

I make it to the beachside courtyard just as Latith walks out from behind the bar. 'Ahhhhh, hello, Mrs Dasha.'

He looks as if he'd seen a ghost.

We awkwardly air-kiss each other's cheeks.

He asks in a perfunctory manner how I am and how John is.

'John died a year ago. From cancer.'

'Ohhhhh.' He looks at the ground and shifts from foot to foot. 'Very sad.' His T-shirt says ONE FLAG ONE COUNTRY.

I notice a small Sri Lankan national flag impaled on a twig branch of the old crooked tree bent over at a right angle across the courtyard. It survived the tsunami and continues to thrive. I sit down and ask if I can order a lime juice.

'Ahhh, no have.'

'Lemon?'

'Ahhh, no have. Have pineapple, banana juice.'

'Okay, I'll have the pineapple.'

Sitting in a familiar lounge chair at a low courtyard table, I look at the zinc-coloured sea, boiling with a swell that has made surfing impossible, let alone swimming. Being the monsoon season, very few tourists walk along the chaotic main road or the eroded beachfront, which is blanketed by a heavy grey woollen sky.

Latith brings me the juice.

'So same-same here?' I ask, looking around.

He nods from side to side, 'Yes, monsoon time now, so only one guest.' He flicks his head toward a lonely-looking man stretched out on one of the sun lounges facing the ocean.

A new wispy beard makes Latith look older than his 25 years. But he still sports the same mournful, indifferent expression he always wore.

'So, are you married?' I try to fill in the awkward space between us.

'No, no,' he replies, looking embarrassed. 'Maybe next year.'

'Ah, so you have a girlfriend?'

'Yes, yes.' He shifts from one thonged foot to the other, looking at the ground.

'And tell me, who is still here? Jayantha?' I persist.

'No, he gone.'

'Suresh?' I continue.

'He in Dubai. Now only one house boy here because is off-season.'

'And Chef Adith?'

'Ahhh, he left maybe more than two years ago. And how is Lola?' he asks, changing the subject by asking about my daughter.

'Very well. Living in Sydney, she has a good job now. She's very happy.'

Having covered the polite basics, Latith retreats into the kitchen, leaving me to it. Whatever *it* is.

I came halfway around the globe, forced myself to come and sit in this spot, this courtyard, and now I have absolutely no idea why I am here. I feel a devastating desolation, an unutterable sadness that John is not with me.

Have I really travelled so far just to feel bottomless grief?

I sit and watch the slate grey sea, and my eyes flick across to the undercover restaurant pavilion that runs the length of the courtyard. The wooden tables we used have been exchanged for brightly-coloured ones, and one of the restaurant walls is now painted bright green, but is studded with peeling patches. Alongside the courtyard, the wall opposite the restaurant that separates this hotel from the neighbouring one is painted orange. This clash of colours is a long way from the all-white boutique hotel look we'd cultivated, with carefully placed orange accents.

As a featured art piece, a broken surfboard is wall mounted, both pieces forming an arch over the restaurant's toilet entrance. I ponder the significance of a broken board, asking myself whether it's a warning for the uninitiated surfer.

My eyes continue tracing the space and end up at the empty restaurant tables when I see John sitting over there, as he had done every day at breakfast.

An apparition that lasts not even five seconds before fading. Then I understand what has brought me back to Hikkaduwa. I badly needed to see John one more time. But not as he became, ravaged by the disease that killed him. As he was, back when we ran the hotel – firing on all cylinders, an effervescent 'mine host', roaring a loud, ready laugh.

I wanted to recapture the intense pleasure of being together while we lived our extraordinary adventure of running the hotel.

Although it hadn't ended the way we wanted or thought it would, we took it to the limit in seizing the time and opportunity to live out our dream together.

We made something new in our relationship, and with that came profound tenderness in fitting our bodies back into each other.

I'm sure we would never have found that renewal between us without the sultry island adventure we embarked upon, impulsively searching for paradise in Sri Lanka. Or our version of it. Our relationship had not only survived the saga but regenerated and flourished. We rediscovered the exhilaration of loving one other before I lost John forever.

As I sit alone, adrift in my head, sipping pineapple juice, I remember one of our conversations over an early morning breakfast. When I felt most threatened at the height of our Nalinda dramas, John told me that his guiding mantra on mortality came from his comedy guru, George Carlin.

John locked eyes with me and recited:

> Life should NOT be a journey to the grave with the intention of arriving safely in an attractive and well-preserved body, but rather to skid in sideways, body thoroughly used up, totally worn out, fag in one hand, chardonnay in the other, screaming 'HOLY SHIT, WHAT A RIDE!'

He'd certainly done that. No question.

I stay for a few minutes longer, and watch the roiling off-season ocean under the dirty monsoonal clouds, with the small sputtering Sinhalese flag stuck on the gnarled beachside tree.

I slowly stand up and walk back down the hotel's long corridor towards the main road.

John was right. There is nothing to regret.

Sri Lanka remains spotlit in my memory bank as the final chapter in a rollicking, swashbuckling life of high times, good times, low times, sad and bad times, and many, many hilarious adventures in between. With John always at the centre of the circus ring, stage-managing the exuberant chaos of our lives, each of us daring the other to go higher, further, in a constant search for the shock of the new.

And I think we both found out that paradise is for visiting.

It doesn't last forever.

Chapter 24

ACKNOWLEDGEMENTS

Among the many books I read about Sri Lanka to deepen my understanding of this captivating place and culture, I'd like to acknowledge the following that are mentioned:

John Gimlette, *The Elephant Complex* (Quercus Publishing Ltd, 2015 Great Britain); Michelle de Kretser, *The Hamilton Case* (A Vintage Book, RandomHouse Australia, 2004); Samanth Subramanian, *This Divided Island* (Atlantic Books 2016, Great Britain); Robert Gray, an extract from the poem *Malthusian Island,* Certain Things (William Heineman,1993, Australia); Sophie Ruggles, *My Barcelona Kitchen*, (Murdoch Books Pty Limited, 2012); Julian Barnes. *Levels of Life*, particularly 'The Loss of Depth' (Vintage, 2014, London).

Other books that contributed inspiration were:

Paul Harris, *Delightfully Imperfect,* A Year in Sri Lanka at the Galle Face Hotel, (Kennedy and Boyd, Scotland UK); Rory Spowers, *A Year In Green Tea and Tuk-Tuks* (Harper Element, 2007); Juliet Coome and Daisy Perry. *Sri Lanka's Other Half* (Sri Serendipity Publishing 2010); David Robson, *Anjalendran,* Architect of Sri Lanka (Tuttle Publishing, 2009, HK).

I would also like to acknowledge the following songs that have been cited:

Perfect Day composed by Lou Reed, EMI Music Publishing; *Pressure Drop* by Toots and the Maytals, Universal Music Publishing; *Tik Tok* by Kesha alongside Dr. Luke and Benny Blanco, Kobolt Music Publishing/Concord Music Publishing; *Get Up Stand Up* by Bob Marley and Peter Tosh Universal/MCA Music/Wise Music/MushroomMusic/Reservoir; *For The Greater Good Of God* by Iron Maiden, BMG Rights Management; *Don't Leave Me this Way* written by Kenneth Gamble, Leon Huff and Cary Gilbert, originally released by Harold Melvin and the Blue Notes, featuring Teddy Pendergrass, WARNER CHAPPELL Music.

* * *

But most of all I want to acknowledge the following people for their generous contributions to this story becoming a book. After a very long gestation.

My immense and enduring gratitude goes to: Lola Pinder, Sophie Ruggles, Sophia Turkiewicz, Stephen Scheding, Neil Butler, Rick Faulkner, Eddie Piper, Claire Scobie, Jeanne Ryckmans, Nadine Davidoff, Alison Lyssa, Helen Simons, Jon Hawkes, Sue Beale, Nick and Lizzy Murray, Wendy Harmer, Brendan Donohoe, Sue Burrows, Joan Bowers, Belinda Holmes, Alistair Jones, Caroline Attwooll, Murditha Dias, Richard Guilliat, Tone Wheeler, Tom Molomby, and finally huge thanks to the mavens of Valentine Press, April Pressler and Rebecca Cox.

ABOUT THE AUTHOR

Dasha Ross
Photo by Tim Bauer

Born and bred in Melbourne, Dasha is a third generation broadcaster/writer and a graduate of the Australian Film, Television and Radio School. After extensive experience working for most major television networks in Australia – as a reporter, producer and executive producer for programs such as the ABC's prestigious Four Corners and the 7.30 Report – she became a commissioning editor in ABC TV Documentaries.

It was after leaving the ABC, that Dasha and her husband, John Pinder, moved to Sri Lanka to relaunch a surfside hotel.

Returning to broadcasting her most recent production is the ABC podcast The Day I Lost My Mind, recounting an episode of transient global amnesia and examining its relationship to orgasm.

She lives amongst the mermaids, occasional sharks, and human wannabes at Bondi Beach in Sydney.

This is her first book; a love letter to her husband.

www.ingramcontent.com/pod-product-compliance
Lightning Source LLC
Chambersburg PA
CBHW032038290426
44110CB00012B/857